NEWTON

A BEGINNER'S GUIDE

JANE JAKEMAN

Hodder & Stoughton
A MEMBER OF THE HODDER HEADLINE GROUP

Orders: please contact Bookpoint Ltd, 39 Milton Park, Abingdon, Oxon OX14 4TD. Telephone: (44) 01235 400400, Fax: (44) 01235 400500. Lines are open from 9.00–6.00, Monday to Saturday, with a 24-hour message answering service. Email address: orders@bookpoint.co.uk

British Library Cataloguing in Publication Data
A catalogue record for this title is available from The British Library

ISBN 0 340 79995 1

First published 2001
Impression number   10 9 8 7 6 5 4 3 2 1
Year   2005 2004 2003 2002 2001

Cover image supplied by Corbis.
Typeset by Transet Limited, Coventry, England.
Printed in Great Britain for Hodder & Stoughton Educational, a division of Hodder Headline Plc, 338 Euston Road, London NW1 3BH by Cox & Wyman, Reading, Berks.

B
NEW

Acknowledgements

I am very grateful for the scientific assistance of Inigo Fraser Jenkins.

CONTENTS

Early Childhood and Schooldays

BIRTH

On Christmas Day, 1642, Hannah Newton, who had been widowed three months previously, gave birth to a boy who was christened Isaac after his father. The child was so tiny and weak he seemed unlikely to live. 'I was born so little they could have put me in a quart pot and so weak that I was little likely to live the day out', he said in later life. (A quart pot would hold just under a litre, or two pints, which gives us some idea of how frail the baby must have seemed.) The Newton family lived in the Manor House at Woolsthorpe, Lincolnshire and, like many English households of the time, had become prosperous through sheep-rearing, though Isaac's father had no education and could not sign his name. It seems a most unlikely background for one of the greatest scientific geniuses the world has known.

Isaac Newton Junior was born shortly after the death of Galileo (because of a ten-day difference between British and European calendars, by continental reckoning Isaac's birthdate was 4 January, 1643, and Galileo had died on 8 January, 1642). Galileo had suffered imprisonment as a result of his theory that the earth revolved around the sun and his theories had made little impact: scientific beliefs were still essentially medieval. The earth was held to be the centre of the universe and geometry and mathematics had scarcely moved beyond the theories of the ancient Greeks. Science was closely tied to Christian doctrine, because religion was held to provide an answer to all questions and, as Galileo had found, it could be dangerous even to question existing beliefs about the natural world.

BRITAIN AT THE TIME

In 1642, Britain had its own particular problems: it was in the throes of the Civil War, partly fought over religious issues. Seven years after Isaac's birth, King Charles I was executed in London, news of which must have spread even to remote communities such as Woolsthorpe: a few years later the boy was to draw a picture of Charles's head on a wall. It was a turbulent world into which the tiny child at Woolsthorpe was born.

Little Isaac did survive against all expectations, but his childhood was not easy. When he was three, his mother married a 63-year-old clergyman and left the little boy to be brought up by her parents. His mother's departure provoked powerful feelings in the child. When he was 20 years old, Isaac Newton made a list of his own sins, in which he included threatening his mother and stepfather with burning their house down. In later life, Newton seems to have had a deeply neurotic personality, suffering from psychological crises and perhaps parental neglect was at the root of his problems. He never mentioned his grandparents with any affection.The stepfather, Barnabas Smith, died when Isaac was 11, and Hannah returned to live at Woolsthorpe with three small children by her second marriage. Shortly afterwards, Isaac, who had attended a little village day school, began his formal education at the grammar school in the nearby town of Grantham, where he lodged with an apothecary (a pharmacist and medical practitioner), Mr Clarke, and his family.

SCHOOL

The grammar schools specialized in teaching Latin and Greek, which was not as impractical for a future scientist as we may think, because most scientific books and papers of the time were written in Latin and it also provided a universal European language in which scholars could correspond. As for science, the school taught some arithmetic, but Isaac rapidly outpaced anything they could teach him, although at first he was placed low down in the school. He seems to have been a lonely and unpopular child, involved in quarrels and fights, which perhaps he did something to provoke, as he remembered putting a pin in another boy's hat on purpose to prick him.

What the residents of Grantham remembered most about him, however, was his love of mechanical contrivances, which must have enlivened small-town life considerably. He kept his tools in Clarke's attic and modelled dolls' houses for the little girls of the family, but also created elaborate machinery. He made a working windmill, a four-wheeled cart moved by a crank handle as the driver turned it and a lantern which he attached to the tail of a kite. He also filled the house of the tolerant apothecary with almanacs and sundials: he never lost this particular interest and throughout his life preferred to tell the time by looking at a shadow instead of at a clock. At a fair, he brought a **prism** and observed how it affected rays of light.

KEYWORD

Prism: Transparent object, usually triangular and geometrical, with surfaces at acute angles to each other which will affect the light passed through them.

The young Newton was clearly a creature of immense practical and intellectual restlessness, even drawing birds, men, ships and plants on the walls of his room: his chief reading was John Bate's *The Mysteries of Nature and Art*, which dealt with practical experiments in mechanics and art, including creating waterworks and fireworks, sketching and engraving. He experienced historical events through his own strange perspectives: in 1658 Oliver Cromwell, the head of the Puritan republic into which England had been briefly turned, died during a great storm. Isaac was outside, practising jumping, measuring how much further he could jump with the wind behind him than against him.

It is not surprising that when he left Grantham and went home to manage Woolsthorpe Manor and its land at the age of 17, the episode was disastrous. He built model waterwheels instead of minding the sheep, and slipped off to read a book if sent into town to do the marketing. He became quarrelsome at home and displayed outbursts of violent anger towards the servants, probably the result of extreme intellectual frustration at being taken away from school. Fortunately, the headmaster of Grantham Grammar School and Hannah's brother, William Ayscough, had both recognized the child's remarkable abilities, and persuaded Hannah to send him back to the school to prepare for Cambridge University. As one of his early biographers put it: 'His genius now began to mount upwards apace.' In 1661, he was admitted to Trinity College and bought some simple necessities in preparation: a lock for his desk, ink, candles, a notebook and a chamber pot.

* * * *SUMMARY * * * *

- Isaac Newton was born in 1642 at Woolsthorpe, Lincolnshire, England.

- It was a period of strong religious belief and little scientific acceptance.

- Newton's early childhood was lonely and unhappy.

- He was a very inventive child.

- He was educated at Grantham Grammar School, Lincolnshire.

University Life

[Note: The scientific ideas in this chapter are described in more detail in Chapter 7.]

AT CAMBRIDGE

Cambridge University was not the tranquil haven of learning that Isaac might have expected. After Cromwell's death the monarchy had been restored and the University had keenly supported Cromwell and Puritanism. Members of colleges who had supported the old regime were now being thrown out. Newton himself did not have an easy time: he was a subsizar, that is, a poor student who had to act as a servant for the Fellows (the lecturers) and rich students. Since his mother had been left a rich widow at the death of her second husband, it is a mystery as to why her brilliantly promising son was treated in this way. The only help that came to him at Cambridge in fact seems to have been from a Fellow of Trinity College, Humphrey Babington, who was the brother-in-law of Mr Clarke, the Grantham apothecary.

At Cambridge, he had a religious crisis, making fervent lists of his 'sins', which included many seemingly harmless pleasures, such as making pies on a Sunday night and sneaking cherry cake. The Restoration of King Charles II, when the exiled king had regained his crown, had already happened in 1660, and a pleasure-loving atmosphere was acceptable at court and in the country generally. However, Puritanism, with its deep mistrust of the slightest enjoyment, had ruled for the whole of Newton's childhood. It had left its mark on him.

Intellectually, Cambridge University was a stagnant backwater, ignoring European developments. The teaching of physics and astronomy, then called *natural philosophy*, was still centred on the ancient philosophers, especially Aristotle, who held that the sun moved around the earth, which was itself immobile. His theory of movement stated that things move by 'natural motion' in order to reach their 'proper places'. The natural motion of the heavenly bodies (the sun, moon, planets and stars) was perfectly circular. Practical experimentation and recording was discouraged and considered intellectually inferior. European thinkers such as Descartes and Copernicus, who were proposing radical new theories of astronomy and matter, were ignored or reviled. The student Newton therefore had to investigate the scientific world for himself and read independently.

He read Descartes, who questioned the theories of Aristotle, holding, for example, that a planet would naturally move in a straight line and that there must be an invisible force which holds it in its actual path. He also thought that something in circular motion strives constantly to fly out from the centre, like a stone whirled around on the end of a piece of string. These were ideas on which Newton could build. There were others that he would eventually not accept. For Descartes, the universe was composed entirely of pieces of matter, whether so large or conglomerated that they formed the 'heavenly bodies' or so tiny and subtle that they filled the space between them, whirling around. The light of the sun and stars, Descartes held, resulted from the pressure of whirling celestial matter.

Also among Newton's reading were works by Galileo, by the British scientists Robert Boyle and Robert Hooke and the philosopher Thomas Hobbes. The Dutch scientist Christian Huygens made another contribution to the young man's knowledge; it was he who coined the term '**centrifugal** force' for Descartes's idea of the force that makes the piece of stone on the string fly outwards.

KEYWORD

Centrifugal: Moving outwards from the centre.

Newton studied books critically – this was his practice throughout his life – making systematic notes of questions and objections and evolving his own theories. For example, he pointed out that if Descartes's theory of light were correct we should be able to see just as well at night, when the celestial matter would presumably still be having its effect of pressure. The theories of light and colour were of particular interest and he experimented on himself, peering at the sun till he had to shut himself up in a darkened room. He took some of these experiments to dangerous extremes, at one stage pushing a bodkin (a large blunt neeedle) between his eye and the socket to see what the effects were on his vision.

In mathematics, Cambridge may have offered the young Newton some stimulus. In any event, something was to happen there that would affect his future. In 1663, the Lucas Professorship of Mathematics was founded by Henry Lucas, a Member of Parliament and a Fellow (senior member, involved in teaching and supervision of the students) of St John's College, Cambridge. (Stephen Hawking now holds this post.) It was part of a general revival of learning, particularly in the sciences, under Charles II: in the same year, the King gave an official warrant to the Royal Society, the oldest scientific society in Britain, which was officially described as 'The Royal Society for the Improving of Natural Knowledge by Experiments'. Both of these developments would have important personal consequences for Isaac Newton.

He had begun intensive reading in mathematics when a national disaster reached the University. An outbreak of bubonic plague spread throughout the country and in 1665 the Cambridge colleges sent their students home, hoping they would escape the infection. Newton returned to Woolsthorpe. He went back to Cambridge for a few months in 1666, but otherwise spent two years at home, following his own devices. It was during this period that he embarked on his most famous discoveries. He was, by his own account, 'in the prime of my age for invention and minded Mathematicks and Philosophy more than at any time since.' This period has been called his *annus mirabilis*, or year of miracles (although it was really more like two years!).

EARLY SCIENTIFIC WORK AND INVENTIONS

At home in Woolsthorpe, Newton worked on geometric problems, conceiving the theorem of the **calculus**. Most famously, it is from this period that we have the story of his formulation of the law of **gravity**, deduced from observing an apple falling to the ground. What makes the apple fall? Why does it fall to the ground, and not fly off sideways or upwards?

KEYWORDS

Calculus: Means of calculating the area within a curve.

Gravity or gravitation: The attractive force exerted by a mass.

The crucial steps in providing an answer were to suppose, first, that there was a force that affected the apple and then that this force, called gravity, extended beyond the earth, even influencing the motion of the moon and counteracting the centrifugal force which would otherwise fling everything off the surface of the earth. Gravity was like the string that kept the stone from flying outwards. It was a moment of brilliant insight, but the ground had been prepared by intensive study. It is possible that the story of the apple was an invention. In any case, the simplicity of the story is a key to the greatness of Newton's thought, especially his ability to make far-reaching deductions from direct observation.

By the time he returned to Cambridge in 1668, shortly afterwards to be elected a Fellow of Trinity College, the foundations of much of his future work had been laid. In 1669, he was made Lucas Professor of Mathematics. The college seems to have been proud of his extraordinary absent-mindedness, particularly his forgetfulness about mealtimes when he was deep in thought, although, apparently, few students attended his lectures.

His intellectual abilities became famous: his extraordinarily wide-ranging mind encompassed mechanics, theology and astronomy as well as mathematics. His studies extended to chemistry, including alchemy, to having a laboratory and furnaces built for experiments.

His experiments with prisms revealed the nature of light, about which people had speculated since the time of the ancient Greeks. He continued his work on **optics**, giving his first series of lectures on the subject and built a new form of telescope with his own hands. This reflecting telescope solved the problem that had bedevilled previous models, namely **refraction** through the lenses which limited visibility, a problem he overcame by introducing a mirror. The further problem, of the head of the observer blocking out the light to the mirror, was solved by providing a mirror at an angle, deflecting the light sideways. Newton shaped and polished the metal mirror himself. Although his telescope was only six inches (15 centimetres) long, it had the same magnification achieved in telescopes that were six feet (three metres) in length.

> **KEYWORDS**
>
> **Optics:** The study of light and sight.
>
> **Refraction:** Change such as bending or breaking up that happens to a ray of light as it is passed through a substance such as the glass of a lens or a prism.

The telescope was sent to the Royal Society, which bestowed on Newton the honour of being a Fellow. He also submitted a paper on the theory of colours, which was published in the Society's journal. Entitled *Philosophical Transactions*, it became the object of long scientific debates. These were to continue throughout his life. Many of these arguments took the form of 'priority' arguments: other scientists claiming to have thought of Newton's theories first. Most of them can be attributed to envy of the rising star of science.

The work on light and colour theory was eventually to be fully published in his work *Opticks*, but that work took 30 years to appear in print. One of the obstacles was said to have been that the manuscript was accidentally burnt in a fire: Newton had left a candle burning dangerously on his desk when he went out for a walk and his dog, Diamond, knocked it over.

Newton's telescope and his work on light made him famous. In particular, a young German scientist, Gottfried Wilhelm Leibniz, studied his paper, *A New Theory about Light and Colours*, published in 1672. It was with Leibniz that Newton was eventually to have some of the bitterest intellectual debates of his career. Robert Hooke made immediate criticisms, complaining that Newton had stolen some of his ideas and a long feud began between the two men, in which Edmond Halley, later to give his name to Halley's Comet, was to become embroiled. Halley would be one of Newton's few long-term supporters. A happier professional relationship began with the young British astronomer, John Flamsteed, later to become Astronomer Royal, who admired Newton's work, though this, too, later turned sour. Even in the quarrelsome and competitive world of seventeenth-century science, it is remarkable how personally Newton took the arguments with fellow scientists: with Hooke and Leibniz especially, he displayed fury and contempt. He had a solitary, touchy, character. In 1679, his mother, whom he nursed during her final illness, died, intensifying his isolation.

For about 20 years, Newton shared his college accommodation with a friend called John Wickins, who was preparing to become an Anglican priest. Newton's religion was unorthodox: he did not accept the belief of the Holy Trinity, that is, Father, Son and Holy Ghost united in one deity. This could have led to his expulsion from the college, since the University regulations said that all Fellows of Cambridge colleges had to be ordained as priests and conform with official state doctrine, but King Charles II's chaplain obtained a special exemption for him. His relationship with Wickins must have been made difficult by their clash of beliefs and their friendship seems to have ceased when Wickins left Trinity to become a village vicar. Newton stayed alone in his rooms, usually working until the small hours of the morning, rarely sleeping for more than four or five hours and corresponding with other scholars by letter. One attractive story is that he invented the cat-flap, to allow his cat to come and go as it pleased without disturbing him. He simply cut a hole in the door and fastened a canvas flap over it. (The story was embroidered further, claiming that he had cut a large hole for the mother cat and a small one for her kittens.)

During the 1680s, his sheltered world in Trinity College suffered the impact of national events: King James II succeeded his brother Charles II in 1687. James was a Catholic who tried to force Cambridge University to accept a Benedictine monk, without requiring him to take any examinations or swear any oath of loyalty to the Anglican Church. The University resented this interference and Newton, surprisingly in view of the general unworldiness which he had shown up to now, was one of the leaders of resistance to the King. This took real courage: Newton and eight other Fellows were summoned to appear before Judge Jeffreys, who in the previous year had condemned 300 people to death for rebellion. James was removed from the throne in 1688 by an uprising in favour of the Protestant William of Orange and the Cambridge rebels were safe.

EARLY PUBLICATIONS

The year 1687 saw another great landmark: the publication of Newton's most famous book, which was to embody much of the work on which he had laboured in his dedicated and intense fashion. This was *Philosophiae Naturalis Principia Mathematica* ('Mathematical Principles of Natural Philosophy'), usually known as the *Principia*, a massive work divided into three parts. It was written in Latin and set out in very formal terms which made it pretty well inaccessible to non-specialists, although Newton took great care to define all his terms.

Books I and II, which laid the foundation of modern science, set out Newton's three laws of motion (the principles of **inertia**, force and reaction). Here were described concepts such as matter, **centripetal** and centrifugal force, and motion. The third book was devoted to astronomy and linked the propositions set out in the first book to the known cosmos.

KEYWORDS

Inertia: The condition in which matter remains in a fixed state unless altered by an external force.

Centripetal: Moving inwards to the centre.

As well as this rigorous science, however, Newton had been evolving non-mechanical views of the universe, especially from studies in alchemy, that is the semi-mystical chemistry and tradition of knowledge that attempted to change various materials into gold. These views led him to see nature as a living being and the world around him as perpetually in a fluid state of decay and rebirth. His interest in hermetics, the secret knowledge believed to have been bequeathed to the intitated by the mystic deity Hermes of ancient Egypt, also led him along unconventional paths. He spent years studying various religions, learning Hebrew for the purpose and identifying a primal religion as the cult of a God of Nature. He began to write a work called *Theologicae Gentilis Origines Philosophicae* ('The Philosophical Origins of Gentile Theology'), arguing that all ancient peoples worshipped the same 12 gods. The *Origines*, as this is known, was not published until 50 years after Newton's death, and then it appeared in Holland: it contained material that was in total opposition to many contemporary officially received beliefs.

FRIENDSHIPS AND ILLNESS

The publication of *Principia* brought Newton the friendship of the philosopher John Locke, who also shared his interest in alchemy and his unorthodox religious views. This proved to be one of the longer lasting of his friendships.

More fervent was the relationship between Newton and a Swiss mathematician, Fatio de Duillier, who was 20 years younger: possibly homosexual in its physical nature, it was certainly of great emotional intensity. Neither man ever married. Writing to his brother, Fatio commented: 'The reasons I should not marry will probably last as long as my life,' which may refer to his relationship with Newton. In 1689, visiting England at the age of 25, he had met the famous scientist at the Royal Society. Fatio was evidently an ambitious young man, with plenty of bravado and anxious to make a name for himself. Thereafter they met frequently and corresponded when apart. Newton's letters display a degree of feeling that seems to go far beyond the interest he might take in encouraging a promising young scientist. He was deeply affected when Fatio suffered from a bad cold and suggested that the young man should move to Cambridge into a room next to his own. He offered to make him an allowance in case he did not have enough money. But this move did not materialize.

Their close relationship continued for some four years and in 1693 Newton visited Fatio twice in London. But then the affectionate intimacy abruptly came to a close. It seems that Newton had been infatuated and charmed by the young man's admiration. He was too young and inconsistent to be a serious threat to Newton intellectually, along with scientists such as Hooke with whom Newton quarrelled. They also had a mutual interest in alchemy, but Fatio may have spoken too publicly of this, a subject on which Newton observed secrecy and perhaps feared ridicule. Fatio was an unstable personality, suffering from swift swings of mood, changing his plans at the drop of a hat. He had, of course, a great deal to gain from the support of the most eminent scientist in Europe and Newton may have eventually sensed his ambition. The closeness of the relationship was also becoming dangerous. By this stage in his career, Newton had become a public figure, enviously watched by many rivals and if Fatio had moved to Cambridge as planned, they would soon have become the target of homophobic attacks. It should be remembered that homosexuality at this period was not only illegal, it was also very severely punished.

Whatever the causes, the fervour ended, but it brought on a deep depression that seemed to unbalance Newton's mind. He wrote a bizarre letter to Samuel Pepys that he had 'neither ate not slept well this twelve month, nor have my former consistency of mind'. Another strange letter apologized to John Locke for accusing him of trying to embroil Newton with women. These letters bore no relation to reality and both recipients were overwhelmed with anxiety for their friend. Newton wrote again to Locke, saying: 'I had not slept an hour a night for a fortnight and for 5 nights altogether not a wink.' This was in 1693, generally referred to as Newton's 'black year', because of the nervous breakdown which he evidently suffered. But it is possible that it had a chemical cause: in the 1970s, tests on a surviving lock of Newton's hair showed unusually high levels of lead and mercury, probably the result of his alchemical experiments.

As Newton emerged from his illness, whether its causes were emotional or physical, he determined to follow a plan which he had thought about earlier and to leave Cambridge. At the beginning of 1694 Charles Montague, later Earl of Halifax, was appointed Chancellor of the Exchequer. Montague had been a student and fellow at Trinity College and was an admirer of the College's most eminent member. He used his position to get Newton appointed as Warden of the Royal Mint, a post which enabled him to leave Cambridge for London.

* * * *SUMMARY * * * *

- Newton studied at Cambridge University, England.

- At home during 1665–6, he discovered the principle of gravity, it is said from watching an apple falling from a tree.

- He invented the reflecting telescope and studied light.

- He became the most famous scientist of his time, revolutionizing physics and astronomy with his unified system of mechanics.

- He studied alchemy and he had unconventional religious beliefs.

- His best-known works are *Principia Mathematica*, in which he described his theories of gravity and motion, and *Opticks*, in which he described his theories of light.

- He communicated with many famous scientists and philosophers, including Robert Hooke and John Locke.

The Royal Mint and Honoured Old Age

If the course of science had been changing dramatically in the late seventeenth century, so had the city of London and, like Newtonian physics, it leapt from the Middle Ages to modernity. The Great Fire of London in 1666 had destroyed much of the medieval city, including the old cathedral of St Paul's and over 80 other churches. Thirteen thousand houses, mostly wooden and huddled in narrow alleyways, had been consumed in the flames. But commercially, the city was buoyant and became richer still on banking and commerce, the largest city in Europe, with a population of about three-quarters of a million. New stone and brick-built housing, wide streets and improved sanitation took the place of festering old quarters where the plague had thrived. Sir Christopher Wren, like Newton a Fellow of the Royal Society and keenly interested in scientific matters, had created a planned urban environment, a sequence of new churches, arrayed so as to set off the splendours of his new St Paul's.

NEWTON STARTS AT THE MINT
The job of Warden was second-in-command at the Mint, where all the national coinage was produced. The actual production took place in the Tower of London, still surrounded by a water-filled moat, where those in charge of the coinage also had offices and accommodation if they wished. So Newton left University life behind and packed up to move to London.

The Mint employed about 500 people and had its own horse-driven machinery for pressing out the coins. Previous holders of the Wardenship and the current Master, Newton's boss, regarded their posts as sinecures: they just drew their salaries without actually doing any work. Newton immediately set about changing this and change was desperately needed, for matters had got so far that the state of the coinage was actually affecting the country's economy. Newton's brief was to carry out a recoinage: that is, to call in all the old coins and replace them with newly minted ones. Many of the old coins were thin and worn, but a great many more were counterfeits. The practice of clipping – that is, of removing a tiny amount from the edges of a coin and then reshaping it so that the alteration was almost unnoticeable – was rife. The Mint had no system of checking quality and there were great variations in the weight of coins. Although milling or patterning the edges so as to prevent clipping had been introduced shortly before Newton's appointment, it was carried out only in a small ineffectual way. In spite of the death penalty imposed on counterfeiters, it was so easy to do that people were not deterred. Indeed, it occurred on such a scale that the country was actually in danger of bankruptcy, because nobody trusted the coinage and the national reserves were run down almost to the limit, since coins newly minted had been melted down and the bullion (that is, the solid precious metal) smuggled out of the country. There were frequent riots because workers did not trust the cash in which they were paid to be genuine coin of the realm. For a country where banking and commerce were now of prime importance, the situation was dire and nothing was being done to improve matters. Newton's new boss, Thomas Neale, the Master of the Mint, spent most of his time gambling and drinking and collecting a royalty on every ounce of gold and silver that was minted.

The presses at the Mint which stamped out the coinage worked 20 hours a day in two shifts, six days a week. Newton carried out a careful study of all the processes involved in making a coin, calculating how operations could be speeded up. Here, of course, his lightning powers of calculation were invaluable, as they were in dealing with dishonest contractors who supplied metal at inflated prices. For example, he estimated that a pound of alloy (the less valuable material that was mixed with copper, silver or gold to make the coins) should cost seven-and-a-half pence. When a supply company claimed twelve-and-a-half pence, Newton was able to bring them to book. Gradually, as the old coins were called in and the new distributed, trust in the currency of the country was built up. The new Warden was not especially popular, since he himself worked a 16-hour day, studied economics in his spare time and oversaw production like a hawk. Nevertheless, he supported his workers in disputes with the authorities at the Tower. And, as he had done with his scientific studies, he read all the major authorities and made systematic notes. When Neale died in 1699, Newton became Master of the Mint; he was now in receipt of a salary of £500 a year (at Cambridge his pay had been £100 per year, although he also received free meals and accommodation), plus royalties on coinage.

Alongside the distribution of good coinage, Newton saw the other means of protecting the value of the currency as the active pursuit of forgers and clippers. After the major push in the effort of recoinage was over and he had more time away from the Mint itself, he actively set about this. Rather improbably for a man who had led a secluded life in a Cambridge college, he frequented seedy pubs and brothels in order to entrap criminals and meet informants. It was a direct contrast with the solitary intellectual life of academia, and showed a quite different side of his character. Indeed, some may have been repelled by this trait in him, because he was merciless to those who were caught, giving evidence that got ten people condemned to death in a single week. The most famous case was that of William Chaloner, a counterfeiter and a flamboyant character who managed to wangle his way out of prison, but was eventually convicted and executed. Newton and his agents supplied detailed documentary proof of Chaloner's misdemeanours.

COMPANIONSHIP IN LONDON

His new life in London included some companionship for a few years: his young niece, Catherine Barton, came to be her uncle's housekeeper. She was a lively and sociable woman, with a wide circle of friends. She was also famous as a beauty and many believed her to be the mistress of Lord Halifax, who had obtained Newton's job at the Mint for him.

When Halifax died, he left her a considerable inheritance. She subsequently married John Conduitt, who set about recording as much of Newton's life as he could and carefully collected up his papers after his death.

After 1703 he needed to do less work in connection with the Mint. Newton continued with scientific studies and honours came to him. In 1703, after the death of Robert Hooke, Newton was made President of the Royal Society in his place and he flung himself into ordering the affairs of the Society as he had done with the Mint, offending many members of the Society. Queen Anne knighted him in 1705, probably for political rather than scientific reasons since he stood (unsuccessfully) for parliament as a supporter of Halifax. After a long delay, during which old enemy Hooke died, Newton published *Opticks* in 1704, setting out his ideas and experiments with light and colour. Unlike his *Principia*, this new work was clearly written in English and enjoyed a wide popularity with the general educated public, as well as with scientists.

His fame continued to grow and by the 1720s he was a wealthy man, generous towards his many relatives. As his health began to fail, he moved to Kensington, which was then a village outside London, where he was looked after by the Conduitts. In 1727 he died, in such pain caused by bladder stones that his tremors shook the whole bed.

On 27 March he was buried in Westminster Abbey. His monument there, designed by William Kent, was erected four years later. The famous epitaph by Alexander Pope was not recorded on it, but should still find a place in any book about him:

> Nature, and Nature's laws lay hid in night,
> God said, *Let Newton Be!* and all was light.

✳ ✳ ✳ ✳SUMMARY ✳ ✳ ✳ ✳

- Having started as Warden, he was eventually put in charge of the Mint, where he was responsible for the production of the country's coinage.

- He tracked down counterfeiters and was merciless in their treatment.

- He became President of the Royal Society and an internationally respected figure.

- He died in London in 1727 and was buried in Westminster Abbey.

4 Science Before Newton

NEWTON'S IMPACT

To understand the impact that Newton made, we need to know something about the state of science when he began his studies. Essentially, the Middle Ages, with their legacy from ancient Greeks, especially Aristotle, Euclid and Pythagoras, still ruled and the movements of the heavenly bodies were believed to be divinely decreed. Astronomy was still largely astrology, that is, the attempt to predict the influences of the stars on human life. Chemistry was still alchemy, which attempted to turn other metals into gold by magical means. Ideas were fixed.

In astronomy, the ancient and medieval concept of the universe still held sway. This was a **geocentric** scheme, (i.e. with the earth at the centre of everything), probably first developed by Anaximander in the sixth century BCE. This

> **KEYWORD**
>
> Geocentric: With the earth at the centre.

idea was still the basis of the scheme of the Greek astronomer Ptolemy, who made observations at Alexandria in the second century CE, and believed that the stars and planets, and the sun itself, revolved above a stationary earth at their centre, in a complex system of wheels within wheels. Everything moved in perfect circles with uniform motion. Astrology, the attempt to predict an individual's future from a horoscope, sprung from a belief that the movements of the stars affected people on earth.

SCIENTIFIC THEORIES OF THE TIME

Aristotle's concepts of motion divided the world into two: above the earth was the heavenly or celestial sphere, where all the heavenly bodies moved in perpetual circles. On the earth, or in the terrestrial domain, movement was naturally in a straight line. This was still taught in universities in the seventeenth century, where physics, the study of the laws of the universe, was called 'natural philosophy'.

The Greeks had made great developments in mathematics and geometry. Eratosthenes, in the third century BCE, had calculated the circumference of the earth at 24,000 miles. (The modern figure is 23,200.) He calculated the distance from the earth to the sun at a figure only one per cent away from the true figure. Two centuries later, Euclid, known as the father of modern geometry, had collected up earlier theories, including those that had mystical elements concerning the design of the universe, and as far as geometry was concerned the works of Euclid were still the main source of information in Newton's time. (When he was once asked to what use the works of Euclid should be put, Newton gave a rude answer.)

To our minds, there is an obvious problem: why should the ancient Greeks, intelligent people who were able to carry out accurate measurements and calculations, have come up with the idea that the earth was the centre of everything? (It was observable, for example, that certain planets moved in an irregular way – yet they were supposed to be moving in perfect circles.) Was it just because that was the way in which things appeared from the human point of view? Many modern historians hold that it was also because the Greeks had an **anthropocentric** world – that is, they put mankind at the centre of everything.

KEYWORD

Anthropocentric: With humanity at the centre.

This system of belief was not overtaken in the Middle Ages: Christianity reinforced it, because it held that man was at the centre of God's creation. Astrology was of great importance still, although Christianity did not officially recognize it: the effect that the stars were believed to have on the human world was of far greater importance than the objective observation of the heavens. The theory of optics and colours was limited: there were essentially only white and black and colours were all produced by varying degrees of black, although there had been much wrangling since the time of Aristotle as to how many colours there were exactly. As far as formal education was concerned, the medieval universities endorsed ancient Greek learning. But gradually, at the time of the Renaissance or rebirth of learning in the sixteenth and seventeenth centuries, these traditional views of the way in which the world worked were being challenged.

The European voyages of discovery involved new observations of the stars, from the decks of the journeying ships and it became indisputable that the earth is a globe. The Arabic understanding of algebra, as it spread to the west, aided calculation, and the astrolabes (instruments for showing the positions of the sun and the bright stars) that they created added to western knowledge.

The biggest challenge to the old order came in 1543 with the publication of *On the Revolutions of the Heavenly Spheres*, by Nicolaus Copernicus (1473–1543). 'Copernicus' is actually a Latin form of his Polish surname, Koppernigk. He studied mathematical science at Cracow University, travelled in Italy and later became a skilled doctor of medicine. But it was his astronomical studies that made him famous. In most respects, Copernicus accepted Ptolemy's system. But he put forward a great challenge to it: Copernicus did not believe that the earth was at the centre of the entire universe. Rather, the centre was a point close to the sun. In his scheme, which is much closer to the modern view than the medieval one, the earth and the planets orbit the sun, and the moon orbits the earth. The daily rotation of the earth, giving night and day, is not because the sun is rotating around it, but because the earth itself is turning on an axis. The sun does not take a year to revolve around the earth, as Ptolemy's system had it, but the earth takes a year to revolve around the sun. However, Copernicus still held to the view that the paths of the planets were perfect circles. During Copernicus's lifetime, his work made little impact. One reason was probably because he was afraid of religious persecution; he kept his work quiet and did not allow his book to be published until he knew he was dying. It was the use that his successors made of it that rattled the bars of the cage in which science was imprisoned.

KEPLER AND HIS LAWS OF MOTION

Johann Kepler (1571–1630), though his hands had been crippled and his eyesight damaged by an attack of smallpox when he was four years old, succeeded in becoming one of the leading astronomers in Germany. He published a book called *Cosmographic Mystery* half a century after Copernicus's work had appeared, which repeated Copernicus's ideas. But the real advance was made soon after this in Prague, when Tycho Brahe (1546–1601) invited Kepler to work with him as his assistant. Emperor Rudolph II was a keen patron of both artists and scientists in Prague and his court provided a centre for the exchange of ideas. Brahe, Danish by birth, was Rudolph's official mathematician and he had an observatory in Prague. In 1572 he had observed a new star in the constellation Cassiopeia and its appearance was another nail in the coffin of Aristotle's outdated system, since that taught that the heavens were fixed and unchanging. Brahe died a year after Kepler had arrived and the young man inherited both his equipment, which included very accurate instruments, and the data of his observations.

In 1609, Kepler formulated three laws of planetary motion:

1 The orbits of the planets are **ellipses** and the sun is one **focus** of the ellipse.

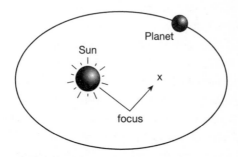

Kepler's First Law No. 1: Planets orbit in an ellipse, with the Sun at one of the foci.

2 If the sun and a planet were joined by a straight line, the line would map out equal areas in equal amounts of time.

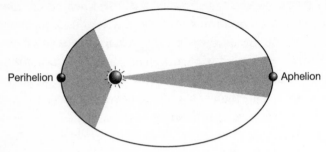

Kepler's Second Law: The shaded parts are equal in area because as a Planet moves round the ellipse, a line joining it to the Sun would mark out equal areas in equal times. Perihelion: the point in a Planet's orbit which is closest to the Sun. Aphelion: the point furthest from the Sun

3 The time taken for a planet to complete an **orbit** and the radius of its orbit are related by a simple formula: the square of the time taken for an orbit is proportional to the cube of the planet's distance from the sun.

KEYWORD

Orbit: The path or track of a circle or ellipse.

The international movement of scientists to overturn received belief continued. The telescope had been invented in Holland in about 1600, but it was Galileo who developed it in Italy. Galileo Galilei (1564–1642) was born and studied at Pisa. Later, he became Professor at Padua and then moved to Florence. The observations he was able to make as a result of the new telescopes were powerful new evidence for the laws that Kepler had deduced. He observed the moons of Jupiter revolving around their planet and was able to show that their paths were elliptical, repeating in miniature the movements of the larger bodies. He also observed the moon through the telescope and decided that its surface was covered in craters. People had previously thought the dark blotches on the moon's surface were of a different colour: Galileo showed they were shadows cast by mountains. In classical astronomy the moon had been assumed to be a perfect sphere with no bumps or craters. His ideas included the proposition that a moving object will keep on moving unless there is some counteracting force that will slow it down, and he seems to have hovered around the idea of a gravitational force without actually formulating such a concept. He investigated the speed of falling bodies, dropping objects from the Leaning Tower of Pisa, noting that similarly shaped objects of different **masses** dropped at the same time, accelerated at the same rate and hit the ground at the same moment (again, this was contrary to Aristotle's teaching) and also that the path of a projectile falling back towards the earth was in a parabolic (a particular form of open curve) line.

> **KEYWORD**
>
> Mass: The quantity of matter that an object or body contains.

Kepler lived in a more tolerant part of Europe, protected by Rudolph and his successor. The ideas of Galileo were a challenge to the Roman Catholic Church's teaching and were denounced by papal authorities. In 1616 the Church officially declared that to believe that the sun is the centre of the universe and that the earth rotates on its own axis was heretical, punishable by death. Galileo was summoned to Rome. He was arrested and forced in 1633 to recant his famous claim that the sun rotated around the earth. Nevertheless, his 'heresy' continued to spread; it had been published in 1632, in his book, *Dialogue on the Two Great Systems of the Universe*, which had been acclaimed throughout Europe.

DESCARTES AND HIS THEORIES

The most important link between Galileo and Newton was the work of the French philosopher, René Descartes (1596–1650). Cartesian physics, as it is known after him, saw nature as a machine and explains everything in terms of mechanical laws, that is, how matter behaves under various forces. In the *Principles of Philosophy*, published in 1644, he set out sweeping new explanations of movement and matter. He held that a body will tend to remain at rest or to move in a straight line, so that the path of a planet would be straight, unless there were some other force that kept it going round. He also saw the universe as created originally by God from matter that broke down, forming the heavenly bodies. Space was actually filled with tiny invisible particles of matter. Gravity was caused by spinning celestial matter, which pushed outwards under centrifugal pressure, being forced back. Light resulted from the pressure of this matter.

Descartes also devised the basic concept of analytical geometry, which enables the drawing of graphs, so that, for example, distance can be plotted against time and shown as a curve to demonstrate variation of speed.

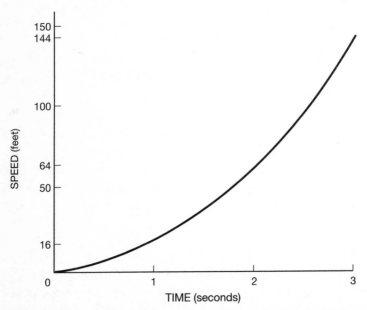

Distance and time: a curve plotted on a graph using Cartesian coordinates. If an object is dropped from a tower, the distance it falls can be plotted against the time it takes to fall. The curve demonstrates the acceleration of the speed of fall.

This theory was published in an appendix to Descartes's *Discourse on Method*, published in 1637 and it caused great excitement in mathematical circles throughout Europe, reaching English scientists such as Isaac Barrow, who held the Lucas Professorship of Mathematics at Cambridge when Newton was a student. Although Descartes was officially disapproved of in Cambridge, Newton read his works extensively. In Europe, the young Christian Huygens, (1629–1695) born in Holland and for a time resident in France, with whom Newton would later have much correspondence, also began to study the Frenchman's publications.

In England, Francis Bacon (1561–1626), a great scholar and statesman, had also been a keen philosopher of science. He believed that searching for the causes of phenomena could greatly increase our control over the natural world. He was an early and powerful advocate of the importance of experiments.

These members of the international intellectual community were Newton's most important predecessors.

✳ ✳ ✳SUMMARY ✳ ✳ ✳

- In ancient and medieval times, people believed that the earth was flat and the sun, moon, planets and stars all revolved around it. This was still taught in the universities when Newton was a student.

- Some scientists before Newton, especially Galileo, who claimed the earth revolved around the sun, challenged the old ideas. Kepler had studied the planets and their orbits.

- Descartes believed that everything was created from large or small pieces of matter and space actually consisted of invisible particles. He held that all the universe obeyed mechanical laws of motion.

- People generally believed that white and black gave rise to all other colours, which were shades in between them.

- The only telescopes available before Newton were clumsy and inefficient, although Galileo had improved the design.

5 Newton's Relationships with Contemporary Scientists

In Britain, the most prominent older scientists when Newton began his studies were probably Robert Hooke and Robert Boyle. Boyle (1627–1691) was an Irishman who had studied the work of Galileo in Italy and had moved to Oxford in 1654, where he began experiments with air pumps, publishing his work on the properties of air in 1660. His famous 'Boyle's law' states that the volume of a gas varies inversely to its pressure. He investigated the expansion of freezing water and the effect of air on sound. Although he is famous as a physicist, chemistry was his favourite study and he became deeply involved in alchemy. He suggested that all matter was 'corpuscular', that is, it consisted of corpuscles of various sorts, even if they were invisible, which could arrange themselves into groups, each of which constituted a chemical substance. Newton studied his work and they became correspondents and friends.

HOOKE

Robert Hooke (1635–1703) helped Boyle in the construction of his air pump. Like Boyle, he was an early member of the Royal Society, where he became Curator of Experiments. This involved organizing several demonstrations to be given each week. He was also a professor of geometry, experimented with optics and dabbled in many fields. He had an extremely quarrelsome nature and tended throughout his life to claim, with any new discovery, that he had thought of it first. He was to claim that he had discovered the law of gravity first. He had in fact suggested that the planets were kept in place by a centre of attraction. He also came up with the idea that this force diminished inversely to the square of the distance between, but without developing the idea as Newton was to do. Sometimes Hooke's claims may have been partly true, but he seems to have had something of a grasshopper mind and his ideas were rarely worked out. Unlike Newton, he was unable to concentrate at great length on a problem. His personality was quite different from Newton's: he was very sociable, loved talking over coffee or port and was keen on sex.

Hooke began to attack Newton's paper on optics and also claimed to have invented a reflecting telescope first. It was the start of a long enmity. So far from contributing positively to the other's work, Hooke and Newton tried to tear one another apart. Hooke claimed that in the *Opticks*, Newton argued that light was 'corpuscular', composed of actual bodies, physical in nature, an idea we have met in the theories of Boyle, but which seemed absurd when applied to light. In fact, he showed little understanding of Newton's explanation that white light is composed of the spectrum of colours. Newton demolished Hooke's criticism without much difficulty, but Hooke clung to the theory that there were only two primary colours, and he put forward a sketchy theory in his book, *Microcosmographia*, that light might be transmitted by pulses or waves. Newton himself, in later life, stated there was nothing in his work that was inconsistent with the wave theory.

HUYGENS

Worse was to come: Christian Huygens, who had been one of Newton's supporters, turned against him. Huygens was one of the best mathematicians in Europe and had built his own telescope. He held his own theory of light as being transmitted in waves and objected to the suggestion that it might be composed of physical bodies. And, whereas Newton had carefully identified seven separate coloured rays, Huygens suggested that there might be only two colours, yellow and blue, from which all the others, even white, were composed. The difficulty was probably caused less by the content of Newton's paper on light than by his approach: this was one of testing a hypothesis by experiments and discarding the theory if the experiment shows it is wrong. Huygens's approach, like that of Descartes, was based on purely theoretical grounds and he did not carry out any experiments at all to disprove

Newton's theory. This was the approach of the older generation of scientists and Newton's insistence on experiment was an innovation. Newton reacted angrily to Huygens's objections and he and the senior European expert on the subject of light ceased to correspond on the subject. Newton offered to resign from the Royal Society, so intense were his feelings, but things settled down somewhat and he did not do so.

LEIBNIZ AND OTHER ASTRONOMERS

With the German scholar, Gottfried Wilhem von Leibniz (1646–1716), another of Newton's long feuds began. Leibniz evolved a pre-atomic theory in which the universe was composed of basic elements which he called *monads*, individual centres of force. 'The monads are the very atoms of nature, the elements of things.' This was to some extent an inheritance from certain ancient Greek philosophers who had held that everything was composed of minute atoms. But Leibniz's monads were active forces in a constant state of alteration and they were also in accord with one another. Thus the universe was in a perpetual state of change, but it was harmonious and all the separate substances in existence are interrelated and form one universe. These concepts clashed with Newton's view of the way in which the universe operated according to universal laws.

The real spat, however, was in a 'priority argument' over which of them had first developed the calculus theory. Although Newton had worked on this when he was a student and composed his book on the subject in 1670–71, it was not published till after his death. But he did show manuscripts of his unfinished works to friends and fellow scientists. In 1684 Leibniz published a work on the calculus, without acknowledging any debt to Newton. He was a brilliant mathematician and had developed the theory quite independently of Newton, but he had seen some of Newton's manuscripts on the subject and that was enough to be accused of plagiarism. Much bitterness followed.

It is sad to sum up these relationships as leading more often than not to quarrels and feuds. With younger men, or those less deeply scientifically involved, and whom he presumably felt were less threatening, things seem to have been easier. Edmund Halley (1656–1742) observed the path of the comet that appeared in 1682, calculated its elliptical orbit, and predicted its return in 1757 – the first time such a prediction had been made. He became professor of geometry at Oxford and later Astronomer Royal. He encouraged Newton throughout the mammoth task of writing the *Principia* and became a long-term friend. With another British astronomer, John Flamsteed (1646–1719), also a student at Cambridge, there were problems: Flamsteed, who suffered poor health, delayed publishing his astronomical observations, which Newton and Halley felt were necessary for the advancement of science.

The philosopher John Locke (1632–1704) was another colleague. Locke had supported Cromwell and the Puritans and was driven into exile in France and Holland for a time after the restoration of Charles II, although he was able to return to Britain in later years. In politics, he held that the first duty of a government was to serve its people, a belief that Newton shared. Locke studied astronomy, chemistry and medicine but, again like Newton, he was also interested in religious questions. The way in which the human mind understood the universe was of deepest importance to him. His *Essay Concerning Human Understanding* (1690) considered the relationship between our thought processes and the material world around us. For Locke, Newton's 'natural philosophy' – his understanding of the way in which the laws of the universe operated – represented an important development from Descartes: he called him 'the incomparable Mr Newton'. Newton's was an empirical view of the universe, that is, one which believes in evolving universal scientific laws by testing and experiment rather than through theory. Locke was not an especially good mathematician and Newton had to provide him with a simplified version of the theory of gravity set out in the *Principia*. Locke's inability to compete in this sphere may have made him a more acceptable friend for Newton than a scientific rival.

Physics, mathematics and astronomy were breaking out of their medieval moulds. All the major European scientists in these fields had published their works, many in Latin, so that it was possible for Newton to read them. But for chemistry, apart from the studies of Boyle, Newton had largely to turn to works on alchemy. (Boyle had also been a keen alchemist.)

THE LURE OF ALCHEMY

There are two distinct differences between alchemy and modern chemistry. First, alchemy had one primary goal: to turn ordinary metal or other materials into gold. Alchemists pursued a substance known as the 'philosopher's stone', which had the power to make this change. Second, alchemy was closely allied to belief systems, so that, for example, certain colours had special meanings or certain acts had to be performed at particular conjunctions of the planets. In alchemy, traditional practices counted for more than the experiments that are the basis of modern chemistry and systematic observation of experiments was not part of the alchemist's normal work.

In seventeenth-century Britain, alchemy was still widely accepted. A well-known courtier, Sir Kenelm Digby, for example, was a keen alchemist and so was the founder of the Ashmolean Museum in Oxford, Elias Ashmole. Alchemy was practically the only source of information about the analysis and reactions of materials available to Newton and at his death he had a large collection of alchemical books, including Ashmole's six-volume work on the subject. Like astrology, its sources were in the ancient world, handed down through medieval times and much influenced by Arab learning. The body of knowledge thus passed down was believed to derive from the mysterious deity Hermes the Great and was called the hermetic tradition.

In London, a circle of alchemists formed around Samuel Hartlib, a Prussian who had come to live in England in 1625. It tried to relate the principles of alchemy to the mechanical philosophy of Descartes and his followers, thus providing a link between medieval alchemy and the emerging science of chemistry. Robert Boyle was a member of this group.

Alchemy had developed certain processes and equipment that became part of modern chemistry, for example, the process of distillation, the use of solvents, funnels, glass and copper vessels and distillation tubes. It had also, as Newton explained when he was an old man talking to his nephew-in-law John Conduitt, evolved a discipline for its students, 'obliged to a strict and religious life. That study is fruitful of experiments.' He was not interested in the prime goal of alchemy, the production of gold, which was only achieved in conjuror's illusions that could not have deceived a mind such as his. But many of its subsidiary achievements were valuable to him. Additionally, he had probably acquired some conventional chemistry from the apothecary in Grantham where he had lodged as a boy and where medicines would have been prepared. With his usual systematic approach, he began in his twenties to compile a dictionary of alchemy and chemistry, containing about 7,000 words. He kept notebooks of the work he carried out in his laboratory at Trinity College. It is this aspect of his work that most approaches modern chemistry: the careful recording of experiments, giving precise quantities and timings. In the 1690s he wrote his principal work based on alchemy, *Praxis.*

From alchemy, Newton had absorbed some beliefs that contradicted Descartes's view, which had no room for belief or feeling, of the universe as a giant machine. The most important of these rather mystical beliefs was that nature is a living being, working in a constant circle of change as things decay and are reborn. Night and day are seen as periods that allow it rest and air. 'This Earth resembles a great animal, or rather an inanimate vegetable. It draws in **ether**eal breath for its daily refreshment and transpires again with gross fermentation.' Then, too, there were invisible

KEYWORD

Ether: The substance full of tiny invisible particles which was supposed to fill air and space. Formerly spelt 'aether'.

forces, such as magnetism, and the way in which some substances, such as oil, mixed together while others, such as oil and water, would not. Alchemy raised problems that Cartesian physics did not cover.

As well as the astronomers, philosophers, mathematicians and physicists, therefore, we must add the alchemists as profound influences on Newton's thought and work.

※ ※ ※ ※SUMMARY ※ ※ ※ ※

- Newton quarrelled bitterly with some contemporaries such as Gottfried Liebniz and Robert Hooke.

- Edmund Halley, an astronomer, and

John Locke, a philosopher, became close friends of Newton.

- Newton studied alchemy, from which he derived much of his chemical knowledge.

The New Philosophy

PRE-NEWTONIAN PHILOSOPHY

The old philosophy was that of the ancient Greeks, especially Aristotle, whose concepts were described in Chapter 4. Newton radically changed our ideas of the universe and how it worked. He gave us a new concept of nature and our ability to control it.

The word 'physics' comes from *physis*, the Greek word for nature. In Newton's time, the subject was known as 'natural philosophy', that is, the branch of philosophy that studied the natural world. This included not only life on earth, but the stars, the planets and indeed the whole universe. The nature of a thing was not just how it appeared, but the reason for its existence and the purpose of its movements. In a way, this is close to the modern idea of 'doing what comes naturally'. But it was applied to objects, not just to living things and their instincts. It was considered the nature of the moon to grow smaller and bigger, just as it was the nature of a lion to hunt its prey. Everything had its natural motion and the natural motion of everything on earth was towards earth's centre, so that if you dropped a stone off a cliff it would be fulfilling its natural movement as it dropped. The natural movement of things beyond the earth was to rotate around the earth in perfect circles. All this was fixed and unchanging.

The fundamental way in which people thought about these things was changed in the sixteenth and seventeenth centuries by people like Copernicus and Galileo, who thought we could understand the world through science and logic. Newton's laws were added to, or modified, theirs. Newton did not just give us new inventions. He gave us new ideas about nature and our ability to understand and control it. For him, 'Natural Philosophy consists in discovering the frame and operations of nature', in other words, how things actually worked, by observing and calculating.

Newton was remarkable as a philosopher not just because he came up with new ideas. His ideas were translated into an understanding of the way in which the whole world behaved. And so there was a further possibility: that the material world could be controlled by human beings, once we understood how it worked. Newton could also do the calculations that would be needed in a practical way and could measure actual distances, speeds and weights. The whole tradition of mechanical inventions in the west, from the steam engine to rocket science, was made possible by the foundations he laid.

In spite of the way in which he questioned conventional religion, he did not give up ideas of a divine origin for the universe and the way in which everything within it behaved, He asked, 'Whence arises all the order and beauty of the world?' and believed that there was a 'Being incorporeal [without a body], living, intelligent, omnipresent [existing everywhere].'

NEWTON'S PHILOSOPHICAL INSIGHTS

The philosophical insights that Newton applied to his discoveries are the really clever things about his thinking. Although he had such a huge range of ability and was a brilliant mathematician and astronomer as well as a physicist, the basic ideas behind his discoveries were essentially very simple. But no one had thought of them before.

Universal application

As we saw earlier, when Newton saw an apple fall to the ground, he realized that some force must make this happen and he called this force *gravity*. But he then went a step further. He realized that this force would apply not only to a small object like an apple, but to everything, including the moon and the planets. So the immense system of the **cosmos** and the small things around us in everyday life all move in the same basic way. Before this, people had thought that one law could apply to small things and another to huge ones. Following Aristotle, who said that

KEYWORD

Cosmos: The universe as a whole, including space beyond earth.

different rules governed the movements of the planets and the movements of things on earth, they did not believe that there were universal scientific rules which controlled the behaviour of everything.

The mechanical universe

Newton established that we live in a universe in which everything moves according to various forces. Gravity pulls an object one way. Pushing or pulling move it another way. The combination of these forces decides the direction and speed of all movement.

So quite ordinary things in everyday life, as well as complex astronomical observations, or scientific experiments, demonstrate Newton's laws. Fairground rides provide a good example. On the roller-coaster, gravity pulls the cars down the dizzy slopes. The **momentum** that they gather as they go downhill does not stop existing when they get to the bottom of the dip. It sends them zooming up the next slope, to fall and rise again.

KEYWORD

Momentum: Not simply the velocity or speed, but the product of the velocity and the mass of a moving object combined.

Gravity affects plants and trees. Seedlings are usually planted with their stems in the air and their roots in the ground. If you plant them so that they lie along the ground, gravity will cause the roots to grow downwards and the stem will grow in the opposite direction (this is known as geotropism).

As we saw have already seen, these principles of gravity and circular motion also apply on a huge scale: they keep the moon in its path around the earth and the planets in their paths around the sun. But the point here is that Newton's laws can be applied to objects of all sizes: the fairground ride as well as the planets. And they apply to all kinds of materials: to metal machinery, to our bodies, to plants and to the great combinations of gases and matter in space.

Rationalism
Universal application was a big step in the development of rationalism. Rationalists believe that it is not necessary to have a revelation from God to understand how the universe operates. We can work it out for ourselves.

Experimentation
Newton believed that it was not enough merely to claim that there were scientific rules affecting the world. Ideas must be tested by experiments. The kites that he built, the water clock, the telescope, were all practical experiments to see how things would work. He kept track of his experiments in notebooks.

This was new thinking. Before Newton, only Galileo had made real practical tests to see if his theories worked and even he did not carry things as far as Newton. The ancient Greeks observed how things worked and came up with ideas, but then they did not put these ideas to the test. They had an admiration for theory and a distrust of practical work that was inherited and it was only in the sixteenth and seventeenth centuries that this ideas was overturned. Archimedes, who was famous for inventing levers and pulleys, including one system by which a man could drag a ship overland single-handed, actually despised practicalities. The Greek historian Plutarch said that he thought the business of mechanics was 'ignoble and sordid' and was much more interested in theories and ideas that had nothing to do with the ordinary day-to-day matters of life.

The medieval chemists tried out various methods in alchemy, attempting to make gold, but they varied in what they did all the time, not measuring or weighing things accurately. Their work involved experimenting in a limited way, but not keeping careful and systematic records of what they tried out, so that they and others could learn from what had happened.

NEWTON'S WORK WITH LIGHT

Newton's work with light is a good example of how he actually tried out possibilities: he did not just suggest ideas about the way light behaved. With the prism, he studied the way in which rays of light passed through a hole made in a wooden shutter in his room and saw that light was made up of the different colours of the spectrum. He recorded these colours as he saw them, and made a diagram of them in a circular arrangement. This is how he described the experiment:

> In the beginning of the year 1666 ... I procured me [obtained] a triangular glass prism, to try therewith the celebrated phenomena of colours. And in order thereto having darkened my chamber and made a small hole in my window-shuts [shutters], to let in a convenient quantity of the sun's light, I placed my prism at his [its] entrance, that it might be thereby refracted to the opposite wall. It was at first a very pleasing divertisement [entertainment], to view the vivid and intense colours produced thereby, but after a while [I began] to consider them more circumspectly [carefully].

The prism broke up the white light coming through the hole into various colours, what we would also call 'the colours of the rainbow'. It also made the circle of white light into an oblong and it made the part of the oblong coloured blue seem more bent out of shape than that coloured red. He got another prism and put it next to the first, facing the other way, so that the ray of light would pass through them both. Thus, the second prism should reverse the effect of the first. And this did indeed happen: the second prism cast a circle of white light. He had demonstrated by experiment that the light of the sun was made up of different colours.

Previously, of course, people had seen that white light passed through a prism turned into different colours. But these colours had been explained, since the time of the ancient Greek philosopher Aristotle, as changes made to the white light, which was altered by the prism. This was believed to happen in various degrees, so that red and yellow were

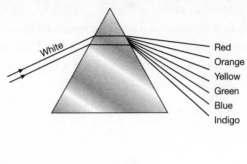

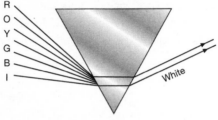

White light passing through a prism. The beam is split up into the component colours, and the experiment can be reversed by passing it through another prism.

believed to be changed the least and green, blue and violet were changed the most. The idea that these coloured lights were already present combined together in the white light, and that the prism was separating them out again was a completely new one. This was not only Newton's theory: he proved it by his experiments with the prisms. They also proved that the different coloured parts of light behaved in different ways, so that, for example, the blue element would bend differently from the red. (There is a reconstruction of this experiment with a prism in Newton's old room at Trinity College, Cambridge, where he carried it out.)

Newton also studied the way in which rings of coloured light appeared to form on either side of two glass plates which are pressed together. He lit them in two different ways: reflected light, that is, a light shone from the same side as the observer, and transmitted light, that is, light shone from the other side so that it passed through the plates. He found that a ring that looked white by reflected light looked black by transmitted light, that red looked blue, that yellow looked violet. He called these pairs 'opposites' and recorded them, and the shades in between them, carefully in diagrams.

The point of all these tests and records is that Newton did not just think up new ideas. He lived in a practical world and tried them out in reality.

THE BEGINNINGS OF MODERN SCIENCE

This was the foundation of modern science, which is based on the rule that you must try out ideas by testing them in experiments, that is, the empirical approach.

Prediction

Newton stated that bodies such as planets, which revolve around the sun, or the moon which circulates the earth, move in certain orbits. These are fixed paths in the form of an ellipse which can be calculated according to mathematical rules or formulae. The set of rules he produced apply to all such bodies, whether we can see them or not, whether they have even been discovered or not.

In Book III of the *Principia*, which deals with astronomy, Newton described comets. He said that some were in orbit around the earth and their paths were very long ellipses. They could only be seen from earth occasionally. But, because they followed this fixed path, they would come round time and time again and it should be possible to predict when they would return. In 1695, his friend Edmund Halley checked through all observations of comets that he could find. He thought that a comet which had been seen in 1682 was very similar to comets seen in 1531 and 1607. This was the comet that had been seen at intervals since the Battle of Hastings in 1066. Halley calculated that it should return in 1758 or 1759. In Paris a French scientist, Alexis-Claude Clairaut, who had helped to translate Newton's *Principia* into

French, did more work on the calculations. He was helped by a woman scientist, Hortense Lepaute. They predicted that the comet should return in mid-April, 1759, plus or minus one month. Huge crowds gathered, staring up at the night sky, as the appointed time drew near – and sure enough the comet appeared, reaching its closest point to the sun on 14 March, 1759. Its latest appearance was in 1986.

Thus Newton's theory about the elliptical orbit of the comet was proved by subsequent events. The law was constant and could be used to predict what would happen.

In a case which confirmed one of Newton's theories long after his death, the planet Uranus was identified in 1781. But when scientists tried to calculate its orbit, they could not get the course the planet was actually following in the sky to agree with the course that would have been predicted according to Newton's methods. Was there something wrong with Newton's theory? But if the astronomers assumed there was another planet, as yet unseen, beyond Uranus, whose gravity was affecting its movements, then the path of Uranus would be correct according to Newtonian science. In 1846, the planet Neptune was discovered and once again a prediction based on Newton's work came true.

Newton's laws are constant: they hold good not only everywhere in the universe, but at all times. So we can predict how objects will behave. Prediction allows machines to be invented, and even rockets sent into space, with the knowledge of how they will behave.

Quantitative science
Newton's laws enabled measurements to be calculated. This was a quantitative approach, that is, it allowed precise quantities of distance, speed, weight, time or other measurements, to be worked out.

For example, his second law of motion (described in the next chapter), which relates to the force used to move an object, stated that acceleration would be proportional to force. This gave a formula from which it was possible to measure the speed of movement and the force used in any particular case. If we know the mass of an object, and any friction to which it will be subject, we can calculate the amount of energy needed to move it.

If two objects come together, we can calculate the force that will be produced. The law of universal gravitation (gravity) states that every particle of matter in the universe attracts every other particle with a force that is proportional to their masses multiplied together. Similarly, we can calculate the force needed to drive two objects apart. This includes the force needed to drive objects away from the earth, that is, to counteract the effect of the force of gravity. So scientists can calculate the amount of energy needed to launch a rocket away from the earth and into orbit and thus know how much fuel will be needed to blast it off.

His discovery of differential calculus enabled measurements of curved shapes and movements in curved lines to be made. This is because it allows calculations to be made where there are different and varying factors such as speed and size.

One of his most remarkable sets of calculations changed the idea of the shape of the earth. Scientists had just come to accept the theories of people such as Copernicus and Galileo, that the earth was a sphere and not flat. But they thought it was a perfect, ball-shaped, globe. Newton calculated the distances from points on the earth's surface at the equator to the centre of the earth. He also calculated the distances from the earth's surface at London and Paris to the centre of the earth. If the earth were really a sphere, like a perfectly round ball, then all these distances should be the same, because all the points on the surface of the earth should be the same distance from its centre. But they are not and Newton worked out that the earth is slightly flattened at the north and south poles. It is shaped more like a tangerine than a perfectly round ball. So ideas of the earth's shape had to be changed somewhat.

The quantitative approach in science is very practical as it means that precise calculations can be made. This allows inventors to estimate what will happen in the real, physical world. We owe achievements from motorcars to space rockets to the ability to actually work out pressures, weights and distances. It may seem an obvious approach to us now, but it was by no means a general way of studying science before Newton.

KEY IDEAS

Universal application: Laws such as gravity apply not only to small objects such as apples but to huge ones such as the planets.

The mechanical universe: We live in a world in which everything that moves acts according to various forces, such as pushing and pulling, which decide the direction and speed of all movement.

Rationalism: It is not necessary to have a divine revelation to understand the universe. We can work it out for ourselves.

Experimentation: Ideas must be tested by experiments.

Prediction: Bodies move according to fixed rules, so we can predict their behaviour in advance.

Quantitative science: We can calculate precise quantities of distance, speed, weight, time and so forth.

* * * *SUMMARY * * * *

Newton's science was philosophically important because:

- It changed people's ideas of how the universe worked by its practical approach.
- The theories are universally applicable, from tiny objects to the planets themselves.
- Newton held that the truth of theories must be verified by experiment.
- He showed that, if a scientific law is correct, it can be used to make predictions.
- His ideas involved the precise measurement of quantities such as speed and distance.

The Great Scientific Ideas

Newton's discoveries can be divided into three groups: in the fields of mechanics, optics and mathematics.

MECHANICS
Newton formulated three major laws of motion: the principles of inertia, of force and of action and reaction. He also formulated the law of gravity. Gravity explains, among other things, the movement of the tides.

First law: inertia
The first law of motion assumed a theory of inertia, that is, an object will remain at rest, or that it will move steadily along a straight line, unless an outside force acts upon it. Objects move through space because there is nothing to stop them. Objects, from planets to particles, can and do attract and repel one another over a distance without anything material between them. In other words, the tiny pieces of matter that Descartes had imagined filled up all the apparent space in the universe, which was traditionally called the ether, were not necessary to transmit force. This is the principle of action at a distance.

Second law: Force and motion
The second law deals with force and acceleration. The force on a body is equal to its mass multiplied by its acceleration. If a **constant** force is applied to something that is stationary, or something that is moving evenly, it will make it accelerate. This can be expressed simply as

KEYWORD

Constant: Not varying; something that does not change.

$$F = ma$$

where F is the force
m the Mass
a the acceleration.

Third law: Action and reaction

The third law, of action and reaction, states that to every action there is always an equal and opposed reaction: if one body exerts a force on another, the second body will exert an equal and opposite reaction on the first.

KEY IDEAS

Inertia: An object will remain at rest or move steadily along a straight line, unless an outside force acts upon it.

Force and motion: The force acting on a body is equal to its mass multiplied by its acceleration (F=ma).

Action and reaction: To every action there is always an equal and opposed reaction.

Gravity: All bodies attract all other bodies: the gravitational force between two bodies can be calculated by multiplying their masses together and dividing the result by the square of the distance between their centres.

THE LAW OF GRAVITY

Newton's 'Universal Law of Gravitation', as he called it, applies to the stars and planets as well as to objects on or near the earth, so it extends from ordinary mechanics to astronomy. Newton demonstrated how gravity acts between two bodies, the apple falling to earth being a simple example of the force pulling the fruit to the ground. To take this a step further, the moon is kept in its orbit around the earth by a balance between gravity pulling it down to the earth and the momentum with which it is travelling. Without gravity, it would fly off: without its momentum, it would fall to earth.

The gravitational force between the moon and the earth is the result of multiplying their masses together and dividing the result by the square of the distance between their centres. The formula for calculating gravitational force is thus:

$$Fg = \frac{Gm_1\, m_2}{d^2}$$

where Fg is the force of gravity
G is the gravitational constant
m_1 is the mass of the earth
m_2 is the mass of the moon
d is the distance between them.

The application of these laws to every known object in the universe meant that a new dimension of scientific research was possible: they eventually provided the basis of the calculations needed to defy the laws of gravity and send objects into space and into orbit.

Newton extended his theories to look at the 'three-body problem', that is, what happens when you have more than just the earth and the moon involved. The sun must also be taken into account, because it also exerts a pull of gravity and is in turn influenced by the other two.

KEY IDEAS

Gravity:

- causes the apple (and other objects) to fall to earth
- causes tidal movements in the seas
- causes the comets to move in their paths
- causes satellites, such as those of Jupiter and Saturn, and earth's own satellite, the moon, to orbit around their planets
- causes the planets in turn to orbit around the sun.

Law of gravity: The force of gravitational attraction between two objects is in inverse proportion to the square of the distance between their two centres.

THE TIDES

The combined effect of the gravitational pulls of the sun and the moon on the waters on earth is responsible for the tides. The influence of gravity thus explained something that had long seemed mysterious. The way in which the level of the sea rises and falls, sweeping rhythmically up a beach and down again, had been observed from ancient times and people had observed that it was somehow connected with the phases of the moon. But it was Newton who laid the foundation of the modern theory of tidal movements.

OPTICS

Some of Newton's experiments with light were described in the previous chapter. He disproved the many previous theories of light that had been put forward by eminent philosophers and scientists including Aristotle, Descartes and Hooke.

To sum up, the generally accepted view when Newton performed his experiments was that colour was created by combinations of light and darkness. Pure white light was changed to red by the addition of a little black. The addition of a lot of black produced blue. Descartes and Hooke had performed experiments: the former had projected a beam of light through a prism held two inches above a piece of paper. Hooke had projected light through a glass of water to a distance of two feet. These were not sufficient to prove anything. Newton, in his rooms in Cambridge, set up his prism so that the beam of light would fall onto a wall and he could see a row of colours: by then passing this through an upside-down prism, Newton reversed the process and thus demonstrated that white light was actually composed of these colours, the spectrum of the rainbow – red, orange, yellow, green, blue, indigo, violet. (You may find 'Richard Of York Gained Battles In Vain' or 'Real Old Yokels Guzzle Beer In Volume' as helpful ways to remember the sequence.)

He set out these colours in a circle and this order has long been the basis of standard colour arrangements, used sometimes by artists to set out paints on their palettes, sometimes by manufacturers of paint and interior decorators. (Sometimes they are reduced to six by counting indigo as blue.) Arranging the colours in this way gave rise to the idea of 'complementary colours', that is, the three primary colours, red, yellow and blue, are each placed opposite colours that are composed of the other two, so that green, made up of yellow and blue, is the 'complementary' of red.

Newton also discovered how the apparently 'white' light had separated into these colours. The beam of light sent through the prism split up into separate rays which were refracted (bent or deflected) to different degrees. He projected the row of colours that came through the prism on to a card with a tiny pinhole in it so that only light from the blue end was allowed to pass through and then so that only red light was allowed to pass through and so on. The blue ray was refracted far more than the red ray. Indigo and violet were refracted most, and the colours at the opposite end, orange and red, were the least affected, while blue, green and yellow were intermediate.

Newton also investigated the substance of light. Descartes had believed that light was a result of the pressure of his 'aether' (now spelt 'ether'), or invisible matter. Colours, according to him, were produced when the particles in the ether rotated. The light was white when they were briskly rotating in the centre of a beam of light, but around the edges, where they were in contact with particles of darkness which were not rotating, their motion slowed down and they appeared different colours, such as red or blue. Newton believed that light was corpuscular, that is, it is made up of many small particles, which enable it to be transmitted through space.

These theories and experiments were to do with the nature of light itself. But they still do not answer the question of why things appear to be different colours. Before Newton, it was generally believed that colour was part of an object. After his *Opticks*, it was possible to understand that the appearance of a colour is caused by the extent to which the object reflects certain parts of the spectrum of light to which it is exposed. If the surface of the object does not reflect any rays at all, but totally absorbs them all, it will appear black.

NEWTON'S TELESCOPE

The telescope that Newton built was another great contribution to the field of optics and to astronomy, for the technique that he used allowed better observation of the heavens. He was not the first to realize that a reflector would be more efficient than a lens at producing an image, because imperfections in the lens distort the image. A Scottish scientist called James Gregory had already thought of the idea of using mirrors instead of a lens, but it was Newton who actually turned it into a success. Furthermore, it supported his theory that light is composed of the different colours of the spectrum: the imperfections in the lenses refracted light, so that colours distorted the image seen through the telescope (this is known as chromatic aberration). When the light was reflected in a mirror, the white beam of light was not broken up in this way, because it bounced off the surface of the mirror instead of passing through it.

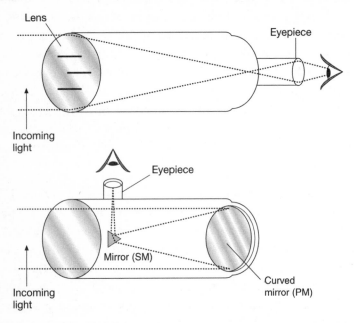

The upper telescope is refracting: light coming through a large lense is bent ('refracted') down the tube to a smaller lens, the eyepiece, which magnifies it.

Below is a reflecting telescope of the type created by Newton: there is a curved mirror at the bottom of the tube which reflects light back to a second mirror, which then reflects the light again up to the eyepiece.

The mirror marked PM (because it is the primary mirror, or the first that the light strikes) is curved. The secondary mirror (SM) is flat, placed at an angle of 45° and reflects the image so the observer can see it.

MATHEMATICS

It was because Newton was a brilliant and original mathematician that he was able to make advances in astronomical theory. Even as an undergraduate, Newton had already begun to make important mathematical advances. Calculations involving infinite series and variable values led eventually to the most famous of Newton's mathematical theories: the discovery of the calculus. Arithmetical calculations, working with fixed measurements, had limited application. Descartes had moved in this direction by bringing algebraic equations into geometry.

A general problem in mathematics at the time was to find the **tangent** to any point on a varying curve, not just on a fixed curve or circle and also the area beneath a curve, to which the same principle can be applied. Newton himself called his method 'fluxions'. The name implies the main feature involved in his discovery: to treat the curve not as something fixed and static but as created by a moving point. Newton built on previous work that considered a curve as being made up by many small **discrete** changes. He could then let the size of these changes shrink towards zero thus modelling the curve to any desired accuracy. The application of this method to variables changing in time was of the greatest importance. It allowed Newton's laws to be applied to complex situations such as the effect of force on a moving body.

The development of these theories by Newton took a long time – it was at least 20 years before the ideas were published. Gravity was something he originally thought operated only on earth: it took time to make the great leap and understand that it was the force that lay behind the astronomical movements that Galileo and Kepler had observed. When he came to look at the relationship between the earth and the moon, Newton had to calculate the momentum (the quantity of motion of something that is moving, calculated by multiplying its mass by its velocity) of the moon and the rate at which it changed. The moon moves in an irregular ellipse, so he had to calculate the speed of an object moving in a variable curve.

The method for finding the tangent to a variable curve is now known as differential calculus. Newton carried his method further to include integral calculus, that is a way of calculating the area under a curve.

ASTRONOMY

The development of this work by Edmond Halley, applying Newtonian mathematics to calculating the orbits of comets, gave astronomy some of its most famous discoveries.

The paths of the comets had been believed by Tycho Brahe to be circular and by Kepler to be straight lines shooting past the earth. There was an especially spectacular comet in 1682 which gave rise to fresh observations. It clearly had a curved path, which suggested that the real orbit might be an ellipse: this meant that it would not go streaking off for ever into outer space, but would at some time reappear.

In 1684 Halley went to visit Newton in Cambridge and asked him what type of curve would be followed by a planet attracted to the sun by the inverse square law of gravity. Newton said that it would be an ellipse and sent Halley a paper (*On the Motion of Bodies in Orbit*) proving the relationship of the law of gravity to planetary orbits. The path of a comet's ellipse could be calculated and the time the comet would take to complete it could be estimated, proving the relationship of the law of gravity to planetary orbits, from the formula which Newton had developed. Halley went through all the records he could find of previous observations of comets and, examining Newton's formula for calculating the time taken to travel the path of an ellipse, was able to estimate correctly that it would return in 1757/8.

Further work by Newton developing the understanding of the forces of gravity produced more valuable astronomical discoveries. He observed and calculated the relationships between the planets Jupiter and Saturn and their satellites. And, by considering the three bodies, earth, sun and moon, he was able to explain changes on or visible from earth. The moon's elliptical path was variable, altering with different pulls exerted by the earth and the sun. These pulls vary as the distance between them varies because the earth does not have a perfectly circular orbit around the sun, so that sometimes sun and earth are further apart than at others.

Also, the force of gravity varies according to which latitude (horizontal division) of the earth you are at. This is because the earth is not a perfectly round ball. As Newton explained to Halley, who wondered why his pendulum clock ran more slowly when he was making observations on the island of St Helena than when he was at home in London, the earth is flatter at the poles and bulges out at the equator. A pendulum clock is operated by a weight which swings backwards and forwards at the same intervals. (It has to be wound up from time to time to keep it going, which is where we get the expression 'clockwork toy', which also has to be wound up.) These intervals move the complicated mechanism that eventually keeps the hands of the clock moving round regularly. But the earth's own gravity operates from the centre of the earth itself, becoming weaker as it moves outwards with the bulge at the equator. So at St Helena, which is nearer the equator than London, Halley's clock was 17 miles further from the earth's centre than London and gravity exerted less influence on the pendulum. The swings of the pendulum, which operated the mechanism of the clock, took longer and the clockface told the wrong time.

KEY IDEAS

Newton discovered:

- differential calculus (finding the tangent to a variable curve)
- integral calculus (finding the area under a curve)
- that the path of a comet is an ellipse
- how to work out when a comet will return
- how to relate the gravitational pulls of the sun, the moon and the earth.

✳✳✳✳SUMMARY ✳✳✳✳

- In mechanics Newton evolved three laws of motion, based on the principles of:
  - inertia
  - force
  - action and reaction.

- In optics
  - he demonstrated that light is composed of the colours of the spectrum
  - he created an advanced reflecting telescope.

- In mathematics and astronomy: he discovered:
  - differential calculus (finding the tangent to a variable curve)
  - integral calculus (calculating the area under a curve)
  - how to calculate the path of a comet.

Science and Society: Newton's Influence on his Own Times

8

NEWTON'S PERSONALITY

We have seen that Newton was a lonely figure, whose personal life contained few friends. He was a sickly child brought up by grandparents and as an adolescent was brilliantly clever but unpopular with other boys. Newton seems to have been the ultimate swot, working on his own until the small hours – there was little place in this life for the pleasures that his contemporaries evidently enjoyed. Coffee houses, for example, the equivalent of modern cafés, were places where many writers and scholars could meet and for the price of a cup of coffee or a modest meal exchange gossip and ideas, read the newspapers, moan about the government and so on. Ale houses, or pubs, had a similar, if more rumbustious, atmosphere, and Cambridge was full of them when Newton was a student there. But there seems little evidence that he socialized in these places: on his visits to London, he caught the stagecoach outside the Rose Tavern, but was far too earnest to linger inside its doors. He did sometimes enjoy a bottle of wine with companions in his college rooms, but even then he had a tendency to forget they were there and bury his head in a book. Even when he took up his job at the Mint and began the business of tracking down forgers, dodging round the most seedy quarters of London, he used informers and agents with whom he did not mix socially. As for closer relationships – wives, lovers – there seems to have been none, except perhaps for the brief passion for Fatio de Duillier, who never shared his life. He was also a touchy and quarrelsome colleague for fellow-scientists. It is impossible to imagine sharing a laboratory with someone so unorthodox and so spiky.

It is all the more remarkable therefore that he occupied a highly respected place in British society. For the country was proud of him, when eventually his achievements became known and he could have been described as a national treasure. Tales of his genius spread. In 1697 Leibniz and a Swiss mathematician, Johann Bernoulli, set up a mathematical problem as a challenge to any European mathematician to try to solve. Other famous mathematicians were unable even to come near an answer. Newton was sent the problem when he was in the throes of his busiest time at the Mint and came home exhausted from a hard day's work. But he had solved it by four o'clock the following morning. He published the answer anonymously, but Bernoulli guessed who had solved it: he said that he recognized 'the lion by its claw'.

The image of Newton popularized science in literary circles. The poet James Thompson, whose long work, *The Seasons*, was first published in sections between 1726-30, included Newton, 'pure intelligence', among great British figures ('Britannia, hail!') and describes the tiny microscopic life in the summer air. And Thomson's lines about light and colour recall the prismatic experiments:

A trembling variance of revolving hues,
As the sight varies in the gazer's hand.

In the London of Newton's day, there was already a foundation of scientific study to which Britain's most famous scientist added lustre and made practical contributions. Gresham College in London had been founded by Sir Thomas Gresham, an Elizabethan merchant and economist, in 1597. He appointed seven professors, including those of astronomy, geometry and physics. Gresham College was the main centre of scientific discovery outside the universities of Oxford and Cambridge before the Restoration of King Charles II.

THE ROYAL SOCIETY

Charles's patronage gave science a leading position in fashionable society. It was considered an appropriate part of a gentleman's education to know something about such matters as gravity, telescopes and air pumps. As well as Gresham College, scientific clubs had been founded in Oxford, Cambridge and London, where new ideas could be discussed and the King's approval set a London group on a strong and fashionable basis. Many non-scientists were members, such as Samuel Pepys, the famous diarist and naval administrator, Edmund Waller, famous as a poet, John Evelyn, the historian and diarist and John Dryden, the playwright. The Royal Society (full title The Royal Society of London for Improving Natural Knowledge) played an important part in spreading information outside the narrow scientific community to a wider middle-class circle. It met in Gresham College and the two institutions had many members in common. In 1665 the Royal Society began publishing a journal called *Philosophical Transactions* which aimed at publicizing discoveries. One of the Society's principal aims was to simplify the language in which science was communicated. Thomas Sprat, who wrote about the Society in 1663, desired a 'natural way of speaking; positive expressions, clear senses; a native easiness, bringing all things as near the mathematical plainness as they can; and preferring the language of artisans [craftsmen and mechanics], countrymen and merchants before that of wits and scholars.'

In reality, the Society communicated to the aristocracy and to the more prosperous middle class and it cannot be said that Newton's *Principia* contributed to ease of understanding, since it was originally written in Latin. The *Opticks*, however, were written in English, and were set out much more clearly. The first English translation of the *Principia*, by Andrew Motte, appeared in 1729, 42 years after its publication in Latin. But Newton was very active within the Society and in this way contributed to its success in spreading scientific knowledge. After Newton became President of the Society in 1703, the first scientist to occupy that position for a long time, there were many quarrels within it, especially a celebrated and bitter one between Newton and John Flamsteed, when Newton was accused of being dictatorial. But its fame increased and many foreign visitors became members. Newton was very active in recruiting them: nearly 100 were elected over a 20-year period, and the fame of British science spread abroad.

When Edmond Halley became Secretary of the Society in 1713, Newton had a colleague with whom he could work constructively. Under Newton's presidency, the Society explored many themes: experiments with air pumps and steam-pumps and the work of Francis Hauksbee which produced electrical impulses by friction. He himself contributed much: in 1704, as President, he presented his second great book, the *Opticks*, to the Society and many lengthy discussions and experiments on the subject followed.

As Newton grew famous he climbed up the social ladder. Knighthood was a big step on the way, and he became influential with Queen Anne and her husband, Prince George, and afterwards with King George I. Partly because of royal interest and partly because of Newton's fame, simplified science became a popular study, discussed in clubs and coffee houses. In addition, the practical demonstrations that Newton organized at the Royal Society attracted much interest. Added to this, Robert Boyle had left money to fund a series of public lectures on the theme of science and religion, all of which were well attended.

POPULAR THINKING AND NEWTON

Perhaps Newton's major contribution to popular thinking was not in any detailed scientific knowledge, but as an approach: accepted truths could be successfully challenged, theories should be tested by observation, records should be kept. During the seventeenth century, although there was still generally a widespread belief in magic, it declined among educated people, because science could explain and show mechanical causes for things that previously seemed to have happened mysteriously. This was especially evident with regard to comets: these had always previously been associated with events on earth and considered as dire predictions of terrible events: one had appeared at the Battle of Hastings in 1066, for example, and was believed to have signalled the defeat of the

English army. Newton's *Principia* dealt extensively with comets. Because some comets had very long elliptical paths, Newton argued, they could be observed only at lengthy intervals, but because they would always take the same time to complete an orbit of the sun, their reappearance was predictable mathematically.

Halley wrote a poem which appeared as an introduction to the *Principia*, which included these lines:

> Now we know
> The sharply veering ways of comets, once
> A source of dread, nor longer do we quail
> Beneath appearances of bearded stars.

It may not be great poetry, but it clearly expresses the feeling that Newton had relieved people from superstition and fear. When he, followed by Halley, demonstrated the elliptical paths of comets, they had shown that there was nothing magical about the date when a comet reappeared: it was simply a matter of calculation. Halley calculated that a comet that had appeared in 1682 was the same one that had appeared in 1607 and 1531 and that it should return to view in 1758/9. There was great popular excitement as people took to the streets to watch for the comet – whose reappearance of course confirmed the correctness of the theories and calculations of Newton and Halley.

Such very visible demonstrations of the power of science had their effect. Rationalism began to replace superstition: astronomy to replace astrology. The Royal Society deliberately took on superstitions and tested them: for example, it was said that spiders could not cross a barrier made from the horn of a unicorn. And there were some objects that were said to be made from the horn of this fabulous creature (they may well have been from rhinos or some other horned animal). At a meeting of the Royal Society, some powdered 'unicorn's horn' was placed in a circle and a spider solemnly put in the middle. The creature crawled out straight away. (A superstitious die-hard could have argued that the test might not have worked because the powdered substance was not real unicorn's horn. But the experiment shows what the scientists were up against when it came to popular beliefs.)

Gulliver's Travels

Of course, the Royal Society came in for its fair share of ridicule, partly as a result of such activities. The new scientific interest was satirized by Jonathan Swift in *Gulliver's Travels*. Swift (like Newton, born after his father's death) knew Newton personally, and seems to have been very much attracted to his niece, Catherine Barton. In spite of this, he made remorseless fun of the Royal Society circle in *Gulliver's Travels* (published in 1726), as it is usually known. The full title is *Travels into Several Remote Nations of the World, in four parts*, by Lemuel Gulliver. One of these 'nations', Lilliput, is well known, of course, as is Gulliver's visit to the Houyhnhms, the kingdom of wise and gentle horses, where humans are the vile and filthy Yahoos. But Gulliver's visit to the island of Laputa is less well known. At the capital of Laputa, Lagado, Gulliver visits the Academy of Projectors, where the professors are busy in experiments such as extracting sunshine from cucumbers. At dinner, the food is served cut into geometrical shapes: 'There was a Shoulder of Mutton cut into an Equilateral Triangle ... The Servants cut our Bread into Cones, Cylinders, Parallelograms and several other Mathematical Figures.'

The inhabitants of Laputa, who had observed 93 different comets, were dreadfully forgetful, parodies of the absent-minded scientist. They were accompanied by servants carrying animal bladders blown up and fastened to sticks, with dried peas or small pebbles inside them so they would rattle. When they wanted to have a conversation, the servant's task was to flap the bladder gently across the mouth of the person who was to speak, to remind them to say something and across the ear of the person who was to hear, to remind them to listen. The entire island floats above the earth, like one of Newton's satellites around a planet, and is guided by giant magnets, in a joke at the expense of the theory of gravity. The book even has a small diagram of the island, a parody of a contemporary astronomical diagram.

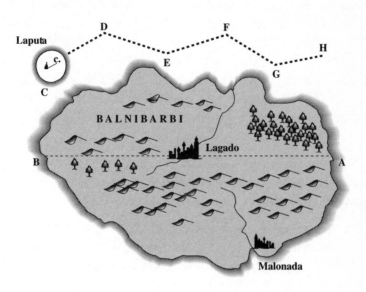

The Island of Laputa in Gulliver's Travels.

This satire was to some extent politically motivated. Swift was a Tory and Newton supported the opposing party, the Whigs. In *Gulliver's Travels*, Swift fantasized speaking to the spirit of Aristotle, who commented very unkindly: 'New Systems of Nature were but new Fashions, which would vary in every age: and even those who pretend to demonstrate them from Mathematical Principles, would flourish but a short Period of Time.' This was clearly aimed at Newton. But Newton's *Principia* was to be no short-lived fashion.

WOMEN'S STATUS IN NEWTON'S TIME

Women could not become members of the Royal Society and in general it was almost impossible for them to get any kind of scientific recognition. Many women had in fact worked on astronomical observations, but usually they were the wives or sisters of male astronomers, who published the results and took all the credit. Tycho Brahe had a sister called Sofie who helped her brother's astronomical work. Maria Kirch, in the late seventeenth century, was married to the most famous astronomer in Germany and worked beside him in his observatory. She discovered a new comet, but the credit went entirely to her husband and after his death she was denied access to the observatory.

Astronomy was particularly difficult for women to study because of the observatories and equipment needed. Theoretical physics and mathematics were easier because they could be studied at home.

In England, Margaret Cavendish, Duchess of Newcastle (1623–1673), took a serious interest in science and wrote six books on physics. But she was refused permission to attend the Royal Society's meetings. It was not until the nineteenth century that a woman was allowed to read a paper to the Society. Another Englishwoman, Elizabeth Carter (1717–1806), who was also a scholar of Greek and Latin, popularized Newton's ideas by publishing a book called *Sir Isaac Newton's Philosophy explained for the Use of Ladies*, which sold well.

In Italy, some women, such as the mathematician and physicist Laura Bassi (1711–1778), did gain recognition in science. She was elected to the Academy of Sciences in Bologna and became a professor, although she was only rarely allowed to lecture. She taught in private, however, and introduced Newton's ideas to Italy.

It was a woman who introduced Newton's ideas to France. Although French scientific societies were no more tolerant towards women than the Royal Society in London, France had an unofficial system which allowed them a much more important role. These were the salons, held in the private homes of wealthy women, where guests were expected to discuss the intellectual matters of the day, including science. The salons were important to the development of science, because they were a means of gaining powerful support and financing. One noblewoman, Émilie, Marquise du Châtelet (1706–1749), mistress of Voltaire, translated the *Principia* into French and added a commentary with many explanations and notes.

It is arguable, that although he had revolutionary ideas in science, Newton did nothing to encourage social change. In spite of his own objections to Christianity, Newton outwardly conformed to the religious standards of his day. Furthermore, although rationalism might be applied to his view of the world, he still believed in the idea of an all-powerful God who had created the universe as a giant machine. This God, of course, was male, and in the order that he had created, woman was an inferior being.

In her book on the role of women in physics, *Pythagoras's Trousers*, Margaret Wertheim puts forward an interesting theory on the influence of Newton on women in society. This is that there was a monastic quality to early science: John Evelyn, one of the founders of the Royal Society, had originally suggested creating an all-male community devoted to science, where the members lived in cells like monks. A number of scientists did in fact resolve to have no sexual relationships: Robert Boyle, deeply religious, took a vow of chastity and his assistant, Robert Hooke, swore that he would never marry. Newton, although there is no record of his having taken such a vow, never in fact married, and there is no trace in history that he ever had a sexual relationship with a woman. In fact, one of the forms that his mental imbalance took was that he was at one time afflicted by the delusion that his friend, John Locke, had involved him in some heterosexual encounter. It is plain from a letter he wrote to Locke about this that the idea of a physical relationship with a woman horrified Newton. 'Being of opinion that you have endeavoured to embroil me with women and by other means I was so much affected with it as that when one told me you were sickly and would not live I answered that it would be better if you were dead.'

That was evidently part of Newton's personal psychological difficulties, but there seems to have been a general feeling in the scientific societies and clubs that the presence of women was contaminating to science. In any case, part of Newton's image as a towering genius was that he was free of any mere physical ties and above any ordinary human bonds.

✳ ✳ ✳ ✳SUMMARY ✳ ✳ ✳ ✳

- Newton became a famous national figure in Britain.

- Because of him, science became popular.

- Newton was President of the Royal Society.

- His science was satirized in *Gulliver's Travels*.

- Women at this time were generally excluded from science.

Newton's Legacy

9

EFFECT ON SCIENCE

We have looked at the effect Newton had in his own time and his influence on those who came after him. But what of his relationship to us – his long-term heirs? It is a complex picture. For, on the one hand, we find a cold, logical approach to science, the legacy of Newton that was most important to the Victorians. On the other, we find a strange mystical aspect, that is probably more interesting from a contemporary viewpoint.

Undoubtedly, Newton gave us the foundation of modern scientific method which insists on testing or observation to prove a theory. To Descartes, Huygens or Hooke, this was not necessary: it was enough to construct an elaborate logical system about the way in which the universe operated without actually examining the natural world or making chemical experiments. This was the normal attitude before Newton. After Newton, it was impossible for a scientist to be taken seriously without producing proof to back up any claims. Inductive reasoning, the process of working out a theory that has dominated science since Newton, is based on this: the scientist sets up a hypothesis and then creates experiments to see whether it can be proved or not. General conclusions can then be drawn from the experiments, as Newton did with his prism and the nature of light. Most of Newton's contemporaries were still using deductive reasoning, a method approved by Aristotle, in which general conclusions were drawn from observations and scientific laws were then deduced, without making experiments to verify them.

In 1989 Professor Fleischmann and Professor Pons claimed that they had produced nuclear fusion, previously only obtainable in advanced research centres, in ordinary room conditions. They termed this cold fusion, because extreme heat was not necessary. But before the scientific world was ready to accept this was possible, many other scientists around the world tested it by carrying out the same experiments – and failed to produce nuclear fusion. Before Newton, the claim of the two professors might have been accepted. After Newton, scientists believe that any claim must be verified by repeating the experiment and seeing if it works.

Nevertheless, our atomic age has taken us away from the nineteenth century. That was a period when Newtonian physics ruled on high, because it was the supreme age of mechanical invention and the guiding principle of Newton had been the practical, hands-on approach. The nineteenth century was the great age of engineering and chemistry, of discoveries in transport and manufacturing and of the empire building overseas that was aided by these technological advances. There is no doubt that the confidence that was so characteristic of the British Empire from Newton's time to the last century came from a view of the world as something that was always measurable, where material problems could always be solved. To the Victorians, Newton was seen as a great rational being, who had made known the principles on which the universe depended. His interests in magic and 'oddball' traditions were ignored.

CONTEMPORARY PICTURE

To us, he has emerged as a rather different figure. For a start, there is his interest in alchemy, which does not deal in rational principles but rather in matters of belief and this makes him a far more complex personality than someone whose thought was always perfectly logical. Then there are his spiritual beliefs: not only his rejection of one of the central Christian doctrines, the belief in the holy trinity, but the theory of ancient wisdom in which he came to believe which was close to many controversial ideas put forward today, for example ideas about the pyramids. Newton believed that ancient civilizations had built their great monuments, such as stone circles and pyramids, as representations of the universe. In about 1000 BCE, King Solomon had created the Temple at Jerusalem. According to Newton, it reproduced the universe and was intended as a pattern for the future. He made plans of the temple, based on references to it in the Bible. He believed that the future of the world could be read in the geometrical arrangement of the temple and created a chronology of the world based on it. He predicted the Second Coming of Christ to be due in 1948 and, more hopefully, that the fourth and fifth centuries of our present millennium will see the beginning of a thousand years of peace.

Recently, we have begun to understand this strange and mystical side of Newton and two recent biographies have stressed it. Betty Jo Dobbs, in *The Foundations of Newton's Alchemy*, described his enormous learning in alchemy and the ways in which it probably inspired many scientific discoveries. Michael White's *Isaac Newton, the Last Sorcerer*, includes a discussion of whether the plan of the Temple of Solomon could have inspired Newton in his grasp of the laws of gravity. We do not see the same clear distinction as the nineteenth century between rational chemistry and irrational alchemy.

Newton himself was a man of great complexity. On the one hand, he was a creature of extraordinary logical and rational thought, determined that theories must be verified by experiment and that the operations of the universe could be explained in practical terms as if it were a giant machine. It is this aspect of his thought that made him a leading light of the philosophy known as British or English Empiricism (nothing to do with the British Empire, by the way!) This was the basic belief of his friend John Locke, who held that all our knowledge derives from experience. This experience is of two types: physical sensation, which tells us about the outside world, and reflection, which is an interior process and provides knowledge of the interior working of the mind. Locke was a close and influential friend of Newton, who certainly shared to some extent in this fact-based view of the human spirit. But at Cambridge he had also encountered a group of thinkers called the Cambridge Platonists, especially a philosopher called Henry More, also a student of alchemy.

The Cambridge Platonists continued the traditions of Neo-Platonism, where mythical and astrological views of the ancient Greeks had been overlaid by mystical beliefs from the Orient and the Middle East. Indeed, Newton certainly had a mystical, religious dimension to his thought, which was deeply influenced by More. More believed that the world was permeated by spirit, which he termed the spirit of nature. This was an invisible force that operated between God, the ultimate controller of everything, and the physical world in which we live. Plato had believed in the notion of spirit as an essence in all things. In human beings it was the soul. It was an extension of God, a force in nature that guided the universe. This would not mean that Newton's laws were invalid: merely that there was a divinity beyond them controlling everything. This rather vague spiritual dimension to Newton is something that is appreciated more in our time than in the last century, when the 'hard-edged' version of Newton as the utterly rational mind was more popular.

More also believed in an early version of atomic theory, that all matter was composed of minute particles that could not be further subdivided. Newton underlined this in his notebook. But at the time he and More believed that these atoms were the proof that God existed, because they must have been created and ordered originally by God. Atomic theory was therefore, for them, part of a religious doctrine. So we cannot say that it affected modern atomic experimentation.

The idea of these invisible particles, which had also been part of Descartes's concept of the universe, did, as we have seen, affect theories of how light worked. It was the start of a long debate in the physics community about whether light was corpuscular (made of particles) or a wave in some medium (such as the ether.) Some time after Newton the wave theory became more popular and was considered to offer a better explanation of observed phenomena. During the twentieth century, with the advent of quantum mechanics, physicists found it necessary to treat light as *both* a wave *and* a particle.

APPLICABILITY OF NEWTON'S LAWS

When it comes to mechanics and practical science, Newton's laws can still be used today, for example, in space science. Astronauts are blasted out into space by the force of a rocket and then, provided the blast does not drive them out into space, instead of continuing on a straight line, they will go into orbit around the earth. There is often a popular misconception of what orbit really means and why astronauts experience weightlessness. Gravity is constantly making them accelerate towards the earth, but if their speed forward (along the tangent) is just right it will carry them around the earth at the same altitude. They are always in free fall (like being in a lift if the cable breaks) and so are weightless, but their forward speed means that they never actually get any closer to the earth. Newton's laws of motion still provide the basis of the calculations needed.

Since 1905 Einstein's theory of relativity has changed the basic assumptions of physics and has overthrown much of Newton's system. In Newton's universe space and time were absolute: that is, they were fixed and all observers could agree on distances measured between points and time durations measured between events. In effect, space and time were the theatre and stage on which planets and stars moved. In Einstein's universe, however, space and time are affected by the objects in them. They are relative, that is to say, they may appear differently to different observers. One of the more startling insights of Einstein is that in a very fast spaceship, clocks would slow down because time is dilated. Furthermore, gravity affects space and time so that near a massive object like the earth time runs more slowly. A consequence of this is that a clock on the the top floor of a high building runs faster than a clock on the ground floor (not because there is anything wrong with the clocks but because of time itself).

Thus Einstein's physics overthrew Newton's laws of gravity, not just in the sense that Newton's law will sometimes give the wrong answer (such as in predicting the complex orbit of Mercury) but in a more radical way – it has a different philosophical foundation.

However, one of the more remarkable features of scientific theories is that even if we know the answer to be literally untrue we can still sometimes continue to use it as an approximation. For nearly all events on earth (that is, at relatively small scale and low speed) Newton's laws can still be used for accurate prediction.

So some of Newton's great theories have at last been overthrown. And, for our ecology-conscious age, the mystical believer in a spirit that infuses all nature is perhaps closer to our emotional needs than is the superhuman logician.

But one legacy has not changed: he never tamely conformed, whether it was to the King's demands to put a royal favourite into Cambridge or the hallowed traditions of Aristotle's views of the world. Probably the most lasting effect of Newton's thought, however, in all fields of life, is the right to question everything.

＊＊＊＊SUMMARY ＊＊＊＊

- Newton gave us the foundations of the modern scientific method that insists on testing everything.

- He was a complex personality with spiritual ideas as well as scientific logic.

- Einstein's theory of relativity overthrew basic Newtonian theory.

- Newton's physics is still used for practical purposes, except for calculations involving immensely long distances or very high speeds.

- In all areas, he questioned everything.

TIMELINE

Newton's Life

1642 Newton born in Woolsthorpe Lincolnshire.

1649

1650

1658 Schoolboy Newton is practising simple experiments.

1660

1661 Newton goes to Trinity College, Cambridge.

1662

1665 Newton graduates from Cambridge and returns to Woolsthorpe to avoid the plague.

1665 'annus mirabilis' – the year of
–66 wonders, during which Newton conceives the idea of gravity and performs early experiments with light and optics.

1666

1667 Newton becomes a fellow of Trinity College.

1669 Becomes Lucasian Professor of Mathematics.

1671 Builds the reflecting telescope.

1672 Becomes Fellow of the Royal Society.

1674

1675

1685

1687 'Principia Mathematica' published.

1688

1696 Newton becomes Warden of the Mint. Moves to London.

The Outside World

Galileo dies. Civil war breaks out in England.

Execution of King Charles I. The Commonwealth begins in England. Oliver Cromwell become Lord Protector (Head of State)

Death of Descartes

Cromwell dies. Night of the 'Great Storm'.

End of Commonwealth. King Charles II restored to throne.

Boyle formulates laws governing pressure of gases.

Plague raging in London and spreading to the countryside.

The English name New York after James, Duke of York, brother of Charles II.

Great Fire of London.

In Holland, Van Leeuwenhoek identifies minute organisms through his telescope Greenwich Observatory founded in London.

Charles II dies and is succeeded by his brother, James. Rebellion breaks out.

James II exiled. William and Mary become joint rulers.

Glossary

Anthropocentric With humanity at the centre.

Calculus Means of calculating the area within a curve.

Centrifugal Moving outwards from the centre.

Centripetal Moving inwards to the centre.

Constant Not varying, something that does not change.

Cosmos The universe as a whole, including space beyond the earth.

Discrete Separate, detached.

Ellipse A flattened circle.

Ether The substance full of tiny invisible particles which was supposed to fill air and space. Formerly spelt 'aether'.

Focus (plural **foci**) Central point of a circle. In an ellipse, one of two points. The sum of the distances to the foci from any point on the ellipse is constant.

Geocentric With the earth at the centre.

Gravity or **Gravitation** The attractive force exerted by a mass.

Inertia The condition in which matter remains in a fixed state unless altered by an external force.

Mass The quantity of matter that an object or body contains.

Momentum Not simply the velocity or speed, but the product of the velocity and the mass of a moving object combined.

Optics The study of light and sight.

Orbit The path or track of a circle or ellipse.

Prism Transparent object, usually triangular and geometrical, with surfaces at acute angles to each other which will affect the light passed through them.

Refraction Change such as bending or breaking up that happens to a ray of light as it is passed through a substance such as the glass of a lens or a prism.

Tangent Straight line touching a curve.

Further Reading

WORKS BY NEWTON

The Principia Bernard I. Cohen, Anne Whitman and Julia Budenz (eds), University of California Press, 1999. Available in paperback and hardback.

The Principia Prometheus Books, 1995. The eighteenth-century translation reprinted in paperback.

The Mathematical Papers of Isaac Newton D.T. Whiteside (ed.), Cambridge University Press, 1967–81 (8 vols).

Opticks Dover Publications. A 1950s' reprint but still obtainable.

The Optical Papers of Isaac Newton Alan E. Shapiro (ed.), Cambridge University Press, 1984.

[*Note*: Newton's religious works are in the process of being edited at Cambridge University.]

WORKS ON NEWTON

All was Light: An Introduction to Newton's Opticks A. Rupert Hall, Clarendon Press, 1993.

Isaac Newton, Adventurer in Thought A. Rupert Hall, Cambridge University Press, 1992 (reprinted 2000). A detailed scholarly biography.

Never at Rest: A Biography of Isaac Newton Richard S. Westfall, Cambridge University Press, 1980. Very comprehensive biography.

Isaac Newton, The Last Sorcerer Michael White, Fourth Estate, 1997, 1998. Very readable, emphasizes the importance of alchemy in Newton's thought.

The Janus Faces of Genius: The Role of Alchemy in Newton's Thought Betty Jo Teeter Dobbs, Cambridge University Press, 1992. Concentrates on alchemy, but includes much information about the Neo-Platonists and other philosophical influences.

The Newton Handbook Derek Gjertsen, Routledge, Kegan Paul, 1986. Gives all the facts in handy reference form. Includes many scientific definitions.

SOME GENERAL WORKS

Enlightenment: Britain and the Creation of the Modern World Roy Porter, Viking, 2000. Deals with science and society in the eighteenth century.

Science and Philosophy Past and Present Derek Gjertsen, Penguin, 1989 (reprinted 1992).

Pythagoras' Trousers: God, Physics and the Gender Wars Margaret Wertheim, Fourth Estate, 1997. Fascinating history of women's struggles for recognition in science.

E=mc² David Bodanis, Macmillan, 2000. Based on Einstein's relativity equation, discussing such terms as mass, energy and the speeed of light. Explains modern physics as well as historical aspects.

Websites

The Isaac Newton Institute at Cambridge University maintains an excellent website with many useful links: **www.newton.cam.ac.uk**

Another well-maintained and organized site is by Andrew McNab: **www.Newton.org.uk**

The Royal Society has a website: **www.royalsoc.ac.uk**

All kinds of scientific information is available on the Science Museum's website: **www.nmsi.ac.uk**

Woolsthorpe Manor, Newton's old home, has a page on the National Trust website: **www.nationaltrust.org.uk**

Woolsthorpe Manor is also open to the public. For details, see website as above or telephone/fax 01476 860338, e-mail: ewmxxx@smtp.ntrust.org.uk

Index

CHARLES DARWIN – A BEGINNER'S GUIDE

Gill Hands

Charles Darwin – A Beginner's Guide introduces you to the man whose scientific observations on evolution challenged the religious beliefs of Victorian society, but which are now generally accepted as being perfectly logical. Examine the historical perspective of evolution and the various philosophical questions that arise. No need to wrestle with difficult concepts as key ideas are presented in a clear jargon-free way.

Gill Hands' informative text explores:

- ■ Darwin's background the times he lived in
- ■ the development of the theory of natural selection
- ■ the scientific basis for evolution
- ■ the relevance of his ideas in today's world.

The facts … the concepts … the ideas …

LOUIS PASTEUR – A BEGINNER'S GUIDE

Peter Gosling

Louis Pasteur – A Beginner's Guide introduces you to the life and work of one of the greatest scientists of the nineteenth century. Find out how his discoveries in chemistry, bacteriology and medicine opened up new fields of research, and discover more about the significance and number of accomplishments that have transformed Pasteur into a popular icon.

Peter Gosling's informative text explores:

- Pasteur's background and the times he lived in
- his role in the foundation of bacteriology
- his work on fermentation and pasteurisation
- the development of the germ theory of disease
- his instrumentation in the development of vaccines
- the relevance of his ideas in today's world.

The facts … the concepts … the ideas …

EINSTEIN –
A BEGINNER'S GUIDE

Jim Breithaupt

Einstein – A Beginner's Guide introduces you to the great scientist and his work. No need to wrestle with difficult concepts as key ideas are presented in a clear and jargon-free way.

Jim Breithaupt's lively text:

- presents Einstein's work in historical context
- sets out the experimental evidence in support of Einstein's theories
- takes you through the theory of relativity, in simple terms
- describes the predictions from Einstein's theories on the future of the universe.

The facts … the concepts … the ideas …

FREUD –
A BEGINNER'S GUIDE

Ruth Berry

Freud – A Beginner's Guide introduces you to the 'father of psychoanalysis' and his work. No need to wrestle with difficult concepts as key ideas are presented in a clear and jargon-free way.

Ruth Berry's informative text explores:

- Freud's background and the times he lived in
- the development of psychoanalysis
- the ideas surrounding Freud's work on the unconscious.

The facts … the concepts … the ideas …

JUNG –
A BEGINNER'S GUIDE

Ruth Berry

Jung – A Beginner's Guide gives you the essential facts and concepts behind the 'father of analytical psychology' and his work. No need to wrestle with difficult concepts as key ideas are presented in a clear and jargon-free way.

Ruth Berry's lively text takes you step-by-step through:

- Jung's background and the times he lived in
- the development of Jungian analysis in simple terms and the key concepts and ideas surrounding his work
- the study of dreams and their interpretation
- the archetypal interpretation of popular myths and legends
- the concept of the symbol

The facts … the concepts … the ideas …